# Sower's Seeds of Encouragement
*Fifth Planting*

## by

## Brian Cavanaugh, T.O.R.

Paulist Press
New York  Mahwah, N.J.

*Also by Brian Cavanaugh, T.O.R.*
*Published by Paulist Press*

THE SOWER'S SEEDS
MORE SOWER'S SEEDS: SECOND PLANTING
FRESH PACKET OF SOWER'S SEEDS: THIRD PLANTING
SOWER'S SEEDS APLENTY: FOURTH PLANTING
SOWER'S SEEDS OF VIRTUE (SPIRITUAL SAMPLER)

*Cover design by Nicholas T. Markell; cover illustration inspired by Fran Balles Goodman*

Copyright © 1998 by Brian Cavanaugh, T.O.R.

Library of Congress Cataloging-in-Publication Data

Sower's seeds of encouragement : fifth planting / [edited] by Brian Cavanaugh.
    p.   cm.
  Includes bibliographical references and index.
  ISBN 0-8091-3811-5  (alk. paper)
    1. Homiletical illustrations.  2. Lent.  3. Easter.  I. Cavanaugh, Brian,  1947–
BV4225.2.S58   1998
251'.08—dc21                                    98–18581
                                                    CIP

Published by Paulist Press
997 Macarthur Boulevard
Mahwah, New Jersey 07430

Printed and bound in the
United States of America

# Contents

# Acknowledgments

Again, I am so grateful to all the people who have purchased my first five books—*The Sower's Seeds, More Sower's Seeds: Second Planting, Fresh Packet of Sower's Seeds: Third Planting, Sower's Seeds of Virtue,* and *Sower's Seeds Aplenty: Fourth Planting.* Your letters of interest and encouragement certainly support my feelings that we are a people of stories. Stories and storytelling form the core of our values and beliefs.

I sincerely acknowledge the contributions of Donna Menis in editing the initial draft and providing valuable insights and suggestions. Also I want to acknowledge Maria Maggi, my editor at Paulist Press, for her continued efforts to push, prod, poke and pull this latest volume of stories into being. Donna and Maria are integral members of the *Sower's Seeds* planting team.

# Introduction
## How Shall We Picture the Kingdom of God?

For me, storytelling is an integral part of my preaching ministry. Once, when asked to write an article about storytelling and preaching, I tried to get a "hook" through the wonders of computer technology. I simply keyed in the search phrase "compare AND kingdom" into my computer Bible program. Let me explain a bit further. Mark 4:30 is the actual verse containing this phrase, but what a difference the translations (New American Bible, Revised Standard Version, New American Standard Bible) provided! The New American Standard Bible translates the word *compare* as "picture." *Bingo!* I had my "hook." Storytelling is a way that a preacher can assist the congregation in envisioning a connection involving the biblical word, the stories of their lives and the kingdom of God.

But, stories (and their telling) have applications far beyond preaching as we share them, learn from them and make them our own. Author Janet Litherland says, "Stories have power. They delight, enchant, touch, teach, recall, inspire, motivate, challenge. They help us understand. They print a picture on our minds....Want to make a point or raise an issue? Tell a story. Jesus did it. He called his stories 'parables.'"[*]

Stories, parables, fables, anecdotes, illustrations, etcetera, help us to see the "bigger picture" in life. They help us to understand that there is more to life than our own limited spheres of experience. They create pictures in our minds and open up our imaginations to comprehend a greater dimension of life than we are normally used to experiencing. Stories have

[*]Janet Litherland, *Storytelling from the Bible* (Colorado Springs, CO: Meriwether Publications, 1991), p. 3.

been vehicles over the years to take us to far off places, places we've never experienced ourselves. Jesus, a master storyteller, proved this to his followers by taking them to a place where there is a new way of living, loving and healing—a world that they could never have imagined on their own.

Taking my cue from the Master, I offer this newest collection of *Sower's Seeds* to encourage you to open your imagination to picture a new way of living, loving, laughing, hoping and healing.

# 1.
## The Town Drunk and the Portrait Painter

Anonymous

Hoping to find a few days' work, a traveling portrait painter stopped at a small town. One of his first clients was the town drunk, who, in spite of his dirty, unshaven face and bedraggled clothes, sat for his portrait with all the dignity he could muster. After the artist had labored a little longer than usual, he lifted the painting from the easel and presented it to the man.

"This isn't me," the astonished drunk slurred as he studied the smiling, well-dressed man in the portrait.

The artist, who had looked beneath the drunk's exterior appearance and seen his inner beauty and created dignity, thoughtfully replied, "But it is the man you could yet become."

Jesus is the artist who paints our portraits and shows us who we could yet become.

# 2.
## A Half-Baked Thanksgiving
(adapted)

Edward Hays

The other day there was an article about a newspaper food editor who, on the day before Thanksgiving, received a telephone call from a youthful-sounding woman. The woman asked how long it takes to roast a 19½ pound turkey. "Just a

1

minute," said the food editor as she turned to consult a chart on the office wall. "Thanks a lot!" said the caller—*click*—as she hung up.

That young cook must have served a Thanksgiving feast fit for wild animals. To believe that a turkey that large could be cooked in one minute is a sign of our times. We have *One Minute Managers,* Minute Rice, one-minute this or instant that. What once took days to prepare, now takes only minutes, whether developing a photograph, preparing food or faxing a message across the continent. But some things, like roasting a 19½ pound turkey, still require time.

Friendship takes time; education takes time; meals that are truly holy and wholesome take time—and so does prayer. We Americans are a people who suffer from a great poverty of time. We are always short of time: time to write letters, time to visit with friends, time to enjoy life and time to rest with our Lord. And the near future, especially for middle-class Americans, will find our clocks running faster and faster. With husbands and wives both working, with numerous commitments to the parish, school and community, and with children involved in numerous extracurricular activities, there is less and less quality time within the family. Consequently, we can expect to see, in the coming years, more instant foods and quick worship services.

But just as a 19½ pound turkey baked for only a minute will be a disaster dinner, so will prayers dashed off "on the run." The soul, like the body, knows hunger, and it will not easily be able to digest even a half-baked prayer, let alone some kind of "minute meditation." Delicious prayer, like a properly baked turkey, requires the same first step: the oven must first be preheated to about 450 degrees. One way to preheat the ovens of our hearts to the proper prayer temperature is with the fire of gratitude and thanksgiving and love for God. Failure to do so may result in properly recited but half-baked prayers.

Next, you need to stuff your prayer, before placing it in the heart oven, with generous handfuls of gratitude seasoned with humility, plus a dash of awareness of your created goodness to remind you of who God is. Then, frequently baste your prayer with the fullness of attention, by bringing your mind back again and again from its constant wanderings.

By the way, regarding the correct cooking time, allow at least twenty to twenty-five minutes per pound if you want a royal Thanksgiving feast.

# 3.
## Glory in Brokenness
(adapted)

Eric Hague

Once upon a time, in the heart of the Great Western Kingdom, lay a beautiful garden. There in the cool of the evening, the Master of the Garden went to walk. Of all the inhabitants of the garden, the most beautiful and most beloved was the noble and gracious Bamboo. Year after year, Bamboo grew ever more glorious, conscious of its Master's love and watchful delight, but modest and gentle too. Often, when Brother Wind came to revel in the Garden, Bamboo would cast aside its grave stateliness to dance and play, tossing and swaying and leaping and bowing in joyous abandon, leading the Great Dance of the Garden, which most delighted the Master's heart.

Now one day, the Master drew near to Bamboo filled with a sense of curious expectancy. And Bamboo, in a passion of adoration, bowed its fronds toward the ground in a loving greeting.

The Master said, "O Bamboo, how I love you. I would now like to use you to help me."

Bamboo flung its leafy crown toward the clouds in utter delight. The day of days had come, the day for which it had been created, the day to which Bamboo had been growing,

3

hour by hour. This was the day on which it would find its meaning and purpose. Bamboo's low, rustling reply was, "Master, O Master, I'm ready. Use me as you so desire."

"My Bamboo," the Master said gravely, "I will use you. I will cut you down!"

A great horror trembled and shook Bamboo: "What? Cut me...down! Oh, not that, I pray you, not that. Use me for your joy, O Master, but please don't cut me down."

"Beloved Bamboo," spoke the Master's somber voice, "if I don't cut you down, I can't use you in my plan."

The Garden was pregnant with silence. Wind held its breath. Bamboo bent its proud and glorious leafy crown. A whisper emerged: "Master, if you cannot use me except by cutting me down...then...do your will...and cut."

"Bamboo, beloved Bamboo, I will cut...I will cut your leaves and branches from you too."

"Master, Master, spare me," cried Bamboo. "Cut me down and lay my beauty in the dust, but would you take from me my leaves and branches too?"

"Bamboo, alas, if I don't cut them away, I cannot use you."

The sun hid its face. A butterfly, eavesdropping, glided fearfully away. And Bamboo shivered in terrible expectancy, whispering: "Yes, Master, cut away."

"O my Bamboo," said the Master, "I would yet ask more...to split you in two and cut out your center, for if I cut not so, I cannot use you."

The Bamboo drooped to the ground, "Master, my Master...then split and cut."

So did the Master of the Garden take Bamboo and cut it down and hack off the branches and split it in two and cut out its center. Then lifting gently, the Master carried Bamboo to where a spring of fresh, sparkling water flowed near the Master's dry fields. Then, placing one end of split Bamboo into the spring and the other end into the irrigation channel in the field, the Master laid down his beloved Bamboo. The spring sang a welcome song, and clear, sparkling water surged joyously down the channel of Bamboo's rent body into the waiting fields. Once flooded, rice was planted, the days went by, and new shoots grew. Soon the harvest was ready.

On that day Bamboo, once so glorious in its stately beauty, was yet more glorious in its brokenness and humility. For in its former grandeur Bamboo was life abundant, but in its brokenness it became a channel of abundant life to the Master's Garden.

# 4.
## A Little Parable for Mothers

### Temple Bailey

The young mother set her foot on the path of life. "Is the way long?" she asked. Her Guide said, "Yes, and the way is hard. But the end will be better than the beginning."

The young mother was happy, and she would not believe that anything could be better than these years. So she played with her children and gathered flowers for them along the way. The sun shone on them and life was good, and the young mother exclaimed, "Nothing will ever be lovelier than this."

Then night came, and tempests tossed. The path was dark, and the children shook with fear and cold. The mother drew them close and covered them with her mantle, and the children said, "Mother, we are not afraid, for you are near, and no harm can come to us." And the mother cried, "This is better than the brightness of the day, for I have taught my children courage."

Morning came and there was a hill ahead. The children climbed and grew weary, but at all times she exhorted the children, "A little patience and we are there." So the children climbed, and when they had reached the top they said, "We could not have done it without you, Mother." The mother, when she lay down that night, looked up at the stars and said,

"This is a better day than the last, for my children have learned fortitude in the face of harshness."

The next day brought strange clouds that darkened the earth—clouds of war, of hate and of evil. The children groped and stumbled, and the mother shouted, "Look up! Lift your eyes to the Light." The children looked up and above the clouds they saw an Everlasting Glory. It guided them and brought them beyond the darkness. And that night the mother got down on her knees and prayed, "This is the best day of all, for I have shown my children God."

The days went on, and the weeks and months and years, and the mother grew old. She was tired and bone weary. Her children were now tall and strong and walked with faith and courage. And when the way was hard, they helped their mother; when the way was tough, they lifted her and carried her. At last they came to a hill, and beyond the hill they could see a shiny road and golden gates opened wide.

The mother said, "I've reached the end of my journey. And now I know that the end is better than the beginning, for my children can walk alone, and their children after them."

The children replied, "You will always walk with us, Mother, even when you have gone through the golden gates."

They stood and watched their mother as she went on alone, and the gates closed after her. And they said to each other, "We cannot see her, but she is with us still. A mother like ours is more than a memory. She is a living presence."

# 5.
## Good Samaritan?

Francis X. Meehan

Once there was a farming town that could be reached only by a narrow road with a bad curve in it. There were frequent accidents on the road, especially at the curve, and the preacher would preach to the people of the town to make sure that they were Good Samaritans to the accident victims. And so they were, as they would pick up the people on the road. One day someone suggested that they buy an ambulance to get the accident victims to the town hospital more quickly. The preacher preached and the people gave.

Then one day a councilman suggested that the town authorize building a wider road and taking out the dangerous curve. It happened that the mayor had a farm market right at the curve on the road, and he was against taking out the curve. Someone asked the preacher to say a word about the councilman's suggestion to the mayor and the congregation the following Sunday. But the preacher and most of the people figured that they had better stay out of politics; so the following Sunday the preacher preached on the Good Samaritan gospel and encouraged the people to continue their fine work of picking up the accident victims—which they did.

# 6.
# Now!

### Theophane the Monk

I had just one desire—to give myself completely to God. So I headed for the monastery. An old monk asked me, "What is it you want?"

I said, "I just want to give myself to God."

I expected him to be gentle and fatherly, but he *shouted* at me, "NOW!" I was stunned. He shouted again, "NOW!" Then he reached for a club and came after me, brandishing his club and shouting, "NOW, NOW!"

That was years ago. He still follows me, wherever I go. Always with that stick, always with that "NOW!"

# 7.
# Prisoners of Fear

### Anonymous

A new prison was completed with much of the labor done by the prisoners themselves. The new modern structure was to replace the old prison that had housed many prisoners for over a hundred years. After the prisoners were moved into their new quarters, they spent long and tiring days stripping the old prison of lumber, electrical fixtures and plumbing. Under the supervision of the prison guards, the inmates then proceeded to tear down the old prison walls.

While dismantling the jail walls, they were shocked and infuriated to find that, although mighty locks were attached to the heavy doors and two-inch steel bars covered the windows, the walls had been made out of paper and clay painted to resemble stone and iron. It was obvious to all the prisoners that during their imprisonment in the old prison, a mighty heave or a hard kick would easily have knocked out the walls, allowing them to escape.

For years they had huddled in their locked cells, thinking escape was impossible. Nobody had ever tried it because it seemed that freedom was beyond the reach of any prisoner.

# 8.
# Age and Attitude

### Attributed to General Douglas MacArthur

Nobody grows old merely by living a number of years. People grow old by deserting their ideals. Years wrinkle the skin, but giving up enthusiasm wrinkles the soul. Worry, doubt, self-distrust, fear and despair...these are the long, long years that bow the head and turn the spirit back to dust.

Whether seventy-one or seventeen, there is in every being's heart the love of wonder, the sweet amazement of the stars and starlike things and thoughts, the undaunted challenge of events, the unfailing childlike appetite for what is next in the game of life. You are as young as your faith, as old as your doubts; as young as your self-confidence, as old as your fears; as young as your hope, as old as your despair.

# 9.
# Legend of the Bluebonnet

Anonymous

The Comanche People moaned aloud to the Great Spirit:

"O Great Spirit, our land is dying and we are dying too. Tell us what we have done wrong to make you so angry. End this terrible drought and save your People before we perish altogether. Tell us what we must do so that once more you will send the rain and restore our land to life."

For three days the People prayed this prayer and dancers danced the prayer. And the People waited and waited, prayed and prayed, but no rain came. And it was very hard on the little children and the old folk.

Among the few children who had not died from hunger was a small girl named She-Who-Sits-Alone. Apart from the crowd, she watched her People pray and dance. In her lap she held a doll that she treasured above all things. It was a warrior doll with a bone belt and beaded leggings, and on its head were blue feathers from the blue jay.

She-Who-Sits-Alone spoke to her doll. "Soon," she said, "the elders will go off to the top of the mountain. They will listen to the winds that carry the wisdom of the Great Spirit. Then we shall know what to do once more to make the rains come and restore the earth."

The elders—in accord with what she had told her doll—

9

went to the hills to listen to winds carrying the voice of the Great Spirit. After many sunsets the elders returned and the people gathered to listen to their message.

The elders said solemnly, "The Great Spirit says that the people have become selfish. For years they have taken from the earth but they have not given anything back. So the Great Spirit says that they must make a sacrifice. They must make a burnt offering of their most valued possession. Then the ashes of such offerings will be scattered on the winds to the four corners of the earth. And when this sacrifice is done, the rains will come and life will return to the earth."

The People gave thanks to the Great Spirit for telling them what they must do, and they went back to their tepees to look for their most valued possessions. One warrior said, "What shall I give? I'm sure the Great Spirit does not want my new bow." A woman added, "I know the Great Spirit does not want my special blanket either." And so it went all throughout the village. Everyone had an excuse to keep what he or she valued most.

Except She-Who-Sits-Alone. She held her warrior doll to her chest and at last spoke to it. "It is you the Great Spirit wants, for you are my most valued possession." And she knew what she had to do.

Later that night, when everyone was asleep, She-Who-Sits-Alone crawled out from her blanket, took a lighted stick from the campfire and crept outside. She went to the top of the mountain, placed the lighted stick on the ground, and spoke aloud: "O Great Spirit, here is my warrior doll. It is the only thing I have from my mother and father. It is my most prized possession. Please accept it."

Still holding her doll, she gathered some twigs and fanned up a fire and held her doll near it. She hesitated and tears began to roll down her cheeks. But then she thought of her parents and grandparents and her friends who had died from the hunger, and thrust her doll into the fire.

When the flames died down and the ashes cooled, she scooped them up and scattered them to the four winds. She was now tired. So on the hill she fell asleep without her doll, but with a smile on her lips.

The next morning the sun awoke her. She sat up, rubbed her eyes and looked out over the hill. As far as she could see where her doll's ashes had fallen, the ground was covered with beautiful blue flowers like little bluebonnets. They were as blue as the feathers in her doll's hair.

When the People came out of their tepees they could hardly believe their eyes. They ran to the mountain where She-Who-Sits-Alone was gazing upon the wonderful sight. There was no doubt in their minds. The flowers were a sign from the Great Spirit that they were forgiven. And, then and there, they sang and danced and thanked the Great Spirit. Suddenly in the middle of their song and dance, a gentle rain began to fall. The land began to live again and the people were saved.

From that day on She-Who-Sits-Alone was known by another name, the One-Who-Loved-Her-People. And to this day, every spring in the People's land, now called Texas, the Great Spirit remembers the love of the little girl and fills the valleys with beautiful bluebonnet flowers.

# 10.
# Strings and Bridges

### Anonymous

There is a story about the Melrose Suspension Bridge, which spans the Niagara River in New York and links Canada with the United States.

It is said that the bridge was built in this way: a kite was flown across the river; attached to the kite was a piece of string; attached to the string was a rope, and to the rope was attached a steel cable. The steel cable was then used to get the rest of the bridge in place.

The story of the Melrose Bridge is often used to illustrate how great things often have humble beginnings.

# 11.
## The Fig Tree

David K. Reynolds, Ph.D.

Once there was a fig tree, grown full in the tropical sun. Each day it endured the heat and still provided shade for those who rested under it. It produced abundant fruit, though some of it was too high for some folks to reach. The highest fruit looked so tasty that some people tried to throw rocks at it, to knock it to the ground so that they could sample it. Some birds nested in the tree. They came and went at their own convenience, safe in the strongest of storms.

In time, the tree died. Still, its remains were used by many creatures as a home and resource. Throughout its existence it remained just a fig tree, doing what fig trees do. It didn't wish that it were a pampered citrus tree or a flowering cherry tree. It took the heat and storms that came its way, and it stood there, being useful. After all, what more can you ask of a fig tree?

# 12.
## Take a Child's Hand

Anonymous

When a child thrusts his or her small hand in yours, it may be smeared with ice cream or jelly, and there may be a wart under the right thumb, or a Band-Aid on a little finger. But the most important thing about this little hand is that it is a hand of the future.

This hand someday may hold a Bible or a revolver; play the church organ or spin a gambling wheel; gently dress a wound or tremble wretchedly, grasping a drug needle.

Right now, that hand is in yours. It represents a full-fledged personality in miniature, to be respected as a separate individual whose day-to-day growth into adulthood is your responsibility.

# 13.
# A Letter of Gratitude

Anonymous

One Thanksgiving some years ago, while watching a football game, a successful businessman reflected on his life and thought of all the people who had been influential in helping him become who he was. He decided to write each person a thank-you card telling him or her of his gratitude for their influence on his life.

His fourth grade teacher quickly came to mind for insisting that he and his classmates strive for excellence in every endeavor. She pounded it into her students, be it regarding homework, tests or class projects. So he sent her a thank-you note.

One day, just after the new year, he received a return letter from his former teacher. She apologized for not replying sooner, but stated that his letter took some time getting to her, since she had moved in with her daughter after retiring from teaching grade school for sixty-six years. She told him how thankful she was to have received his card and how it cheered her to find out he had learned so well his lessons in excellence. She went on to say that in her sixty-six years of teaching, this was the first thank-you card she had ever received, and how grateful she was that he had taken the time to remember her.

So who is it that needs to hear from you during this Thanksgiving?

# 14.
# The Sanctuary

Mary Alice and Richard Jafolla

Far into the Arabian desert—so far that few have seen it or even know of its existence—stands a small fortress. In silence and isolation, the sanctuary rises out of timeless sands, ready to offer safety and provisions to anyone who might come upon it.

It is said that Thomas E. Lawrence, better known as "Lawrence of Arabia," found refuge and sustenance in the little fortress on numerous occasions. When under attack, often against overwhelming odds, he would make his way to the remote desert sanctuary. It was his life support, providing him with food, water, safety and the opportunity to regroup, so that when he was ready he could face the world again.

At times, each of us longs for a sanctuary far removed from current challenges and busyness. However, you do not have to go off to a faraway place; you have your own sanctuary—always ready, always waiting. It is the safety, the protection, the peace and the comfort you experience when you enter into conscious communion with God.

Prayer opens the door through which you enter a sanctuary of strength and safety, protection and renewal. Times of prayer, of conscious contact with God, provide you with sustenance and renewed vigor so that when you are ready you can face the world again—uplifted, refreshed and empowered.


# 15.
# The Old Faithful Well

John Sanford

A young boy spent a month every summer with his parents in an old farmhouse. The house was 150 years old when

14

his family bought it. It had never been modernized. The water supply during those years came from an old well that stood just outside the front door. This well was remarkable because it never ran dry. Even in the severest summer droughts, the old well faithfully yielded up its cool, clear water.

The day came when the family sanctuary was modernized. A new well was drilled a few hundred feet from the house. The old well was capped to be kept in reserve.

The old well remained covered for several years until one day, moved by curiosity, the now grown young man decided to uncover and inspect the old well's condition. As he removed the cover, he fully expected to see the same cool, moist depths he remembered so well as a boy. But the well was bone dry.

It took many inquiries to understand what had happened to the well. He learned that this type of well is fed by hundreds of tiny underground rivulets along which seeps a constant supply of water. As water is drawn from the well, more water flows into it along the rivulets, keeping these tiny channels clear and open. But when such a well is not used and the water is not regularly drawn, the tiny rivulets close up. The well, which had run without failing for so many years, was now dry—not because of a water shortage, but because it had not been used.

# 16.
# Worn, Faded and Beautiful

## Stephanie Whitson

The white water pitcher's once bright finish is now dulled with time. Embellished by tinges of brown, a checkerboard pattern of cracks is scattered across the glaze. On one side there is the faint imprint of a bouquet of pink and blue flowers. The scalloped lip of the pitcher dips at one edge, forming a shallow spout. The handle is gracefully curved, and the body widens as it nears the base. The charm of the pitcher lies in the character

15

etched by the years into its finish. The faded bouquet imprinted on its side betrays countless washings. The pitcher has grown beautiful, not by being set upon a shelf in some china cabinet, but by being used over the years. The finish has worn, the flowers have faded and the pitcher has become beautiful, like a face creased by years of laughing.

People, like water pitchers, are made for a particular purpose. God bestows gifts on each of us so that we may enrich the lives of others. With years of service, we become beautiful—not because we have been saved high on a shelf where we cannot be marred, but because we have been used for God's purposes.

## 17.
## No Committees in Heaven

Msgr. Joseph P. Dooley

When God was creating the animals, a group of angels remarked that it looked like fun, so God let them form a committee and create one animal.

The committee created the platypus—an animal with the bill of a duck, the fur of an otter, the tail of a beaver and the feet of a frog.

"Enough!" shouted God, and ever since then there have been no committees in heaven.

## 18.
## Raising the Bell

Anonymous

There is a story about a heavy bronze bell that had sunk to the bottom of a river in China. The efforts of various engineers to raise the bell were to no avail. At last, a clever monk asked for permission to make the attempt, on condition that the bell should be given to his temple. After receiving permission, he then had his assistants gather an immense number of bamboo poles.

Bamboo is hollow, light and practically unsinkable. The poles were taken down by divers, one by one, and fastened to the bell.

After thousands of poles were fastened, the bell began to move, and, when the last one had been added, the buoyancy of the accumulated poles was so great that they actually lifted the enormous bell to the surface.

You may think that your piece of bamboo is too small and too light to make any difference, but it is necessary in God's sight to build up the Body of Christ.

# 19.
# It Began in a Tomb

## Mark Link, S.J.

There is a story about a hardened criminal serving a life sentence, who felt such despair that life no longer had any hope for him. His behavior got so mean that he was sent to solitary confinement for three weeks to what was known as "the Hole."

One day while in "the Hole," a remarkable thing happened. He was laying on the cold cement doing sit-ups when he noticed something was wedged into the back corner of the cell, under the sleeping platform. He had no idea how it got there, but figured a former resident of "the Hole" must have left it. He wiggled it out. It was, of all things, a copy of the New Testament. Now the thing that is so remarkable is that the inmate actually began to read from it.

The inmate had always been a dynamo of power and energy. Suddenly, he began to wonder what would have happened to him had he used his power and energy for good rather than evil. The thought completely boggled his mind. For a long time he lay there thinking:

"Why did God create me? Why did God create someone who would end up behind bars? Why did God create someone who would die to goodness and love and be buried in a tomb of evil and hate in a prison cell?"

What happened next is hard to describe. A surprising thought entered the inmate's mind. The greatest event in history began in a tomb—a tomb just as secure and guarded as his prison cell. That event, of course, was the resurrection of Jesus. Jesus is no longer buried in a tomb. He has been raised from the dead. He now lives. Yes, Jesus lives!

A second thought jolted him. What happened to Jesus in the tomb could happen to him too, in "the Hole." Because of Jesus' new life and glory, he too could be reborn. He too could be re-created. In a sense, he too could rise from the dead.

At that moment something roused deep within him; he felt it stirring. He asked Jesus to come to him and raise him to new life, to re-create a hardened criminal into a new person. And what happened to Jesus in the tomb happened to the prisoner in his tomb, "the Hole." The resurrection power of God brought him to new life.

That man was Starr Dailey, who, after being released from prison, became one of the pioneers of prison reform in the United States.

Do you ever find yourself in a tomb, buried in some hole, like this criminal?

- It may be a tomb of resentment because of some hurt received from others.
- It may be a tomb of fear about the future and what it may hold.
- It may be a tomb of despair about some difficult situation and how to handle it.

Jesus wants to give us the power to rise from our tombs and out of our holes. This is the good news of Easter.

It's the good news that no tomb can hold us anymore—not the tomb of despair, not the tomb of discouragement, not the tomb of doubt, not even the tomb of death itself.

# 20.
# Becoming a Community

Anonymous

As the Persian Gulf War ended and both Kuwait and Iraq rebuilt their shattered countries, more and more of the atrocities that took place in Kuwait during the Iraqi occupation came to light. But, as always, in the midst of the murders, tortures and lootings, there were stories of extraordinary courage and generosity through which the sacredness of humanity triumphed.

Najeeb Bastaki, a twenty-four year-old Kuwaiti living in Kuwait City, was a member of the Kuwaiti resistance. But as he told a reporter, "The word 'resistance' doesn't mean I carried a gun and fought and killed. What we did mostly was get food and money to families that needed it."

The system worked like this: every week, resistance workers would meet at a secret point and collect rice, sugar, butter and other food staples from the main food co-ops, which were underground partners in the arrangement. At night or early in the morning, the resistance members would fan out around the city, delivering to designated homes a "main store"—a shipment of ten sacks of rice, fifty kilograms of sugar, ten cans of butter and so on. Each home that accepted a delivery was responsible for distributing the food to nine neighboring homes.

Money was distributed on a more informal basis, Najeeb explained. "It is our way that no one in need should ever know who gives money. So if you knew a family that needed money, you would just slip out of the house early in the morning and put an envelope under the door....The wealthy people did this. I myself have money, so I did it. I gave away about $10,000."

In the midst of the horrors surrounding them, the Kuwaitis became a community. Through sacrifice, generosity and selfless service, they "resisted" the evil around them.

# 21.
# An Unlikely Prophet

## Barbara Reynolds

Barbara Reynolds wrote in her column "From the Heart" in *USA Today* about the death of Lee Atwater. She quotes Atwater as saying, "My illness helped me to see that what was missing in a society is what was missing in me: 'a little heart, a lot of brotherhood.'"

He had rocketed to fame as Republican National Committee chief, but now he was saying that what really counted was not power, wealth or prestige, but the golden rule.

Atwater, suffering from brain cancer, challenged the nation: "The '80s were about acquiring wealth, power, prestige. I acquired more than most. But you can acquire all you want and still feel empty.

"It took a deadly illness to put me eye-to-eye with that truth, but it is a truth that the country, caught up in its ruthless ambitions and moral decay, can learn on my dime....I don't know who will lead us through the '90s, but they must be made to speak to this spiritual vacuum at the heart of American society, this tumor of the soul."

At the end, Atwater moved from being a political assassin into the realm of an Isaiah-like prophet, calling for the rich and powerful to repent of their excesses and greed. Here is a man whose guidebooks had been Plato's *Republic,* Machiavelli's *The Prince* and Sun Tzu's *The Art of War.* Before he died, he added a fourth guidebook, the Bible.

Lee Atwater left a campaign theme more enduring than any sound bite or bumper sticker: repent and change. Lee died on March 29, 1991, at the age of forty.

# 22.
# Even Teacups Talk

Anonymous

Pick up a children's storybook and you'll be surprised at what you learn. You'll discover that a teacup can tell you a story that could change your life. Consider this paraphrase of one children's storybook.

A grandfather and a grandmother are in a gift shop looking for something to give their granddaughter for her birthday. Suddenly the grandmother spots a beautiful teacup.

"Look at this lovely cup!" she says to the grandfather.

He picks it up and exclaims, "You're right! This is one of the loveliest teacups I've ever seen."

At that point something remarkable happens—something that could happen only in a children's book. The teacup says to the grandparents, "Thank you for the compliment. But I wasn't always beautiful."

Instead of being surprised that the teacup can talk, the grandparents simply ask, "What do you mean when you say you weren't always beautiful?"

"Well," says the teacup, "once I was just an ugly, soggy lump of clay. Until one day someone with dirty, wet hands scooped me up and threw me on a potter's wheel. Then she started turning the wheel faster and faster until I got so dizzy I couldn't see straight. 'Stop! Stop!' I cried.

"But she repeated, 'Not yet!'

"Finally, she stopped. But then she did something even worse. She put me into a furnace. It got hotter and hotter until I couldn't stand it. Again I cried out, 'Stop! Stop!'

"Still she said, 'Not yet!'

"Finally, when I thought I was going to burn up, she took me out of the furnace. Then some short lady began to paint me. The fumes from the paint got so bad that I felt sick. 'Stop! Stop!' I pleaded.

"The short lady too said, 'Not yet!'

"At last she stopped. But then she gave me back and that other woman put me back into that awful furnace. This time it was hotter than before. And I shouted, 'Stop! Stop!'

"The woman peered in and said, 'Not yet!'

"Now, at long last, she took me out of the furnace and set me aside to cool—'Phew.' When I was completely cooled, a young boy put me in a box with straw all over me and other teacups too. Then a pretty lady put me on this shelf, next to the mirror.

"When I looked in the mirror I was amazed at myself. I couldn't believe what I saw. I was no longer ugly, soggy and dirty. Now I glistened. I was beautiful, firm and clean. Oh, how I cried for joy.

"It was then that I realized that all that suffering was worthwhile. Without it I would still be ugly, soggy and dirty. And it was then that all that pain took on meaning and made some sense to me. It passed, but the beauty it brought remained."

# 23.
# Love Brings Trouble

Anonymous

It's been said that when we love people and go out of our way to help them, we become vulnerable. That's what the wealthy industrialist Charles M. Schwab declared after going to court and winning a nuisance suit at age seventy. Given permission by the judge to speak to the spectators, Schwab made the following statement: "I'd like to say here in a court of law, and speaking as an old man, that nine-tenths of my troubles are traceable to my being kind to others. Look, you young people, if you want to steer away from trouble, be hard-boiled. Be quick with a good loud 'no' to anyone and everyone. If you follow this rule, you will seldom be bothered as you tread life's pathways. Except you'll have no friends, you'll be lonely and you won't have any fun!"

Schwab made his point—love may bring heartache, but it's worth it!

# 24.
# Finally, Out to the Ball Game

## Richard Bauman

When you visit a major league baseball park, you can't be sure your team will win. But you *can* be sure, when the bottom of the seventh inning rolls around, you'll be on your feet singing "Take Me Out to the Ball Game."

It may be the most famous song in the world about baseball—or any game, for that matter. But did you know it was written by someone who had never seen a baseball game?

Jack Norworth composed his "ball song" in 1908 when he was thirty years old. Riding the subway one day, he saw a placard with the message, "Come to the Polo Grounds and enjoy a ball game."

"An idea flashed across my mind," he explained. "I figured there had never been a baseball song, so I pulled a hunk of paper out of my pocket and started scribbling. The music and words came together. Thirty minutes later I had it."

But it was thirty-four years later before he saw his first real game. It was 1942 when a friend finally convinced him to watch the Dodgers and Giants at Ebbets Field. "I caught the fever," he said of that first game, and for the rest of his life Norworth was a baseball fanatic.

Yet how could someone who didn't know a home run from a sacrifice bunt write the best known sports tune of all time? "Robert Louis Stevenson wrote *Treasure Island*," Norworth pointed out, "but there was no such place." It was simply a matter of using one's imagination.

# 25.
# Greatness and Humility

Anonymous

On the 27th of March, 1808, a grand performance of *The Creation* took place in Vienna. The composer himself, Franz Joseph Haydn, who was then seventy-six, was able to be in attendance. He was so old and feeble that he had to be wheeled into the theater. His presence aroused intense enthusiasm among the audience, which could no longer be suppressed as the chorus and orchestra burst with full power into the passage, "And there was light."

Amid the tumult of the enraptured audience, the aged composer was seen striving to raise himself. Once on his feet, he mustered up all his strength, and in reply to the applause of the audience, cried out as loudly as he was able, "No, no! Not from me, but," he said, pointing to heaven, "from thence—from heaven above—comes all!"

He then fell back into his chair, faint and exhausted, and had to be carried out of the theater. What a humble acknowledgment for a great musician to make.

# 26.
# Plans or Bridge?

Anonymous

There's an amusing story from General Stonewall Jackson's famous valley campaign. Jackson's army found itself on one side of a river when it needed to get to the other side. After telling the engineers to plan and build a bridge so the army could cross, Jackson called his wagon master in to tell him how urgent it was that the troops cross the river as soon as possible. The wagon master started gathering all the logs, rocks and fence rails he could find and soon built a bridge.

Long before daylight General Jackson was informed that all the troops, wagons and artillery had crossed the river. General Jackson asked where were the engineers and how did they accomplish the task so quickly?

The wagon master's only reply was that they were still in their tent drawing up plans for building a bridge.

# 27.
# Copper Kettle Christians

Anonymous

A woman in Bible study related that when she recently went into her basement, she made an interesting discovery. Some potatoes had sprouted in the darkest corner of the room. At first she couldn't figure out how they had received enough light to grow. Then she noticed that she had hung a copper kettle from a rafter near a cellar window. She kept it so brightly polished that it reflected the rays of the sun onto the potatoes.

She exclaimed, "When I saw that reflection, I thought, I may not be a preacher or a teacher with the ability to expound upon Scripture, but at least I can be a copper kettle Christian, catching the rays of the Son and reflecting his light to someone in a dark corner."

# 28.
# The First Step Is Courage

Anonymous

There is a story related to the Old Testament tradition concerning the Exodus of the Israelites from Egypt. Picture the scene of the Israelite nation led by Moses, fleeing from slavery and bondage. Their Exodus is stopped on the shores of the Red Sea and the people are glancing back over their shoulders. God has promised them liberation and freedom. They know that and they believe it, but now they are standing on the shore of the sea and Pharaoh's army is in hot pursuit.

Moses raises his arms and voice in prayer for God to lead his people to safety. He gestures with his staff over the water, but nothing happens. Indeed, nothing happens until the first person actually steps into the water and shows, through that simple act, that he has faith in God's promise of salvation. When that first step of courage is taken, the sea parts, and the people cross over into freedom and liberation.


# 29.
# World, My Son Starts School Today!

Abraham Lincoln

"World, take my child by the hand—he starts school today! It is all going to be strange and new to him for a while, and I wish you would sort of treat him gently. You see, up to now, he has been king of the roost. He has been the boss of the backyard. I have always been around to nurse his wounds, and I have always been handy to soothe his feelings.

"But now things are going to be different. This morning he is going to walk down the front steps, wave his hand

and start on a great adventure that probably will include wars and tragedy and sorrow.

"To live in this world will require faith and love and courage. So, World, I wish you would sort of take him by his young hand and teach him the things he will have to know. Teach him—but gently, if you can.

"He will have to learn, I know, that all people are not just—that all men and women are not true. Teach him that for every scoundrel there is a hero; that for every enemy there is a friend. Let him learn early that the bullies are the easiest people to lick.

"Teach him the wonder of books. Give him quiet time to ponder the eternal mystery of birds in the sky, bees in the sun and flowers on a green hill.

"Teach him that it is far more honorable to fail than to cheat. Teach him to have faith in his own ideas, even if everyone tells him they are wrong.

"Try to give my son the strength not to follow the crowd when everyone else is getting on the bandwagon. Teach him to listen to others, but to filter all he hears on a screen of truth and to take only the good that comes through.

"Teach him never to put a price tag on his heart and soul. Teach him to close his ears on the howling mob—and to stand and fight if he thinks he is right. Teach him gently, World, but do not coddle him, because only the test of fire makes fine steel.

"This is a big order, World, but see what you can do. He is such a nice son."

Signed: Abraham Lincoln

# 30.
# Warmth of Your Love

## Paul M. Stevens

A Japanese magazine has a picture of a butterfly on one of its pages. The color is dull gray until warmed by a person's hand. The touch of a hand causes the special printing inks to react, and the dull gray is transformed into a flashing rainbow of color.

What other things can be changed by the warmth of your love and your touch? Your family? Your community? Even your city?

The world is hungry for the touch of someone who cares—who really cares! That someone can transform the world.

"Love one another as I have loved you" (John 15:12).


# 31.
# Love: Heaven or Hell

### Anonymous

No one ever said it better than C. S. Lewis: "To love at all is to be vulnerable. Love anything and your heart will certainly be wrung and possibly be broken If you want to make sure of keeping it intact, you must give your heart to no one, not even to an animal. Wrap it carefully round with hobbies and little luxuries; avoid all entanglements; lock it up safe in the casket or coffin of your selfishness. But in that casket—safe, dark, motionless, airless—it will change. It will not be broken; it will become unbreakable, impenetrable, irredeemable....The only place outside heaven where you can be perfectly safe from all the dangers of love...is hell."

# 32.
# We Are Three, You Are Three
## (adapted)

Anonymous

When the bishop's ship stopped at a remote island for a day, he was determined to use the day as profitably as possible. He strolled along the seashore and came across three fishermen mending their nets. In pidgin English they explained to him that centuries before, their people had been Christianized by missionaries. "We Christians!" they exclaimed, proudly pointing to each other.

The bishop was impressed. He asked if they knew the Lord's Prayer. They had never heard of it. The bishop was shocked. How could these men claim to be Christians when they did not know something as elementary as the Lord's Prayer?

"What do you say then, when you pray?" he inquired.

"We lift eyes to heaven. We pray, '*We are three, you are three, have mercy on us.*'" The bishop was appalled at the primitive, downright heretical nature of their prayer. So he spent the whole day teaching them the proper way to say the Lord's Prayer. The fishermen were slow learners, but they gave it all they had, and before the bishop sailed away the next day, he had the satisfaction of hearing them go through the entire prayer without an error.

Months later the bishop's ship happened to pass by those islands, and the bishop, as he paced the deck saying his evening prayers, recalled with pleasure the fact that on that distant island were three men who were now able to pray correctly, thanks to his patient, pastoral efforts. While he was lost in thought, he happened to look across the water and noticed a spot of light coming from the island. The light kept approaching the ship, and, as the bishop gazed in wonder, he saw three men walking on the water toward the boat. The captain stopped the boat and all the sailors leaned over the rails to see this amazing sight.

When they were within speaking distance, the bishop recognized his three friends, the fishermen. "Bishop," they exclaimed, "we so glad meet you. We hear your boat go past island and come hurry hurry meet you."

"What is it you want?" asked the stunned bishop in awe.

"Oh, Bishop," they said, "we so sorry. We forget lovely prayer. We say: '*Our Father in heaven, holy be your name, your kingdom come,*' then we forget. Please teach us whole prayer again."

The bishop felt humbled. "Go back to your homes, my good men," he said, "and each time you pray, say, '*We are three, you are three, have mercy on us!...*' And, if you remember, ask for mercy too on this bishop."

# 33.
# Pain Passes...Beauty Remains

Anonymous

In 1954 the great French painter Henri Matisse died at the age of eighty-six.

In the latter years of his life, arthritis crippled and deformed his hands, making it painful for him to hold a paintbrush. Yet he continued to paint, placing a cloth between his fingers to keep the brush from slipping.

One day someone asked him why he submitted his body to such suffering. Why did he continue to paint in the face of such great physical pain?

Matisse replied, "The pain passes, but the beauty remains."

## 34.
## God Is Love

Anonymous

One day a pastor was walking along a country road with an old-time friend. As they strolled through the farmland, the pastor noticed a barn with a weather vane perched on its roof. At the top of the vane were the words: GOD IS LOVE.

The pastor remarked to his friend that he thought this was a rather inappropriate place for such a message. "Weather vanes change with the wind," he related, "but God's love is constant."

The friend walked along a little farther before replying, "I don't agree with you about those words. You misunderstand the meaning. The weather vane is indicating a truth: regardless of which way the wind blows, God is love, and such love is constant."

## 35.
## Commencement and Parents' Trauma

Erma Bombeck

Humorist Erma Bombeck began a graduation address with these words:

"I know all of you are sitting out there today frightened, scared and apprehensive about your future. You're wondering how you're going to fit into the scheme of things and face the challenges that lie ahead of you. But I'm not here to talk to you parents. I'm here to address your children.

"Graduation day is tough for adults. They go to the ceremony as parents. They come home as contemporaries. After twenty-two years of child raising, they are unemployed. They no longer have to have a stocked refrigerator when they go on vacation. They can buy a new car without worrying whether or not their child is going to need tuition for summer school....They can come and go as they please and not have to check with their kids. They have the opportunity to put into practice all the things they've learned over the past four years...that there is a life after children and bread can be frozen.

"My heart goes out to parents as I see them sitting there, out of a job and wondering how they will handle their new lifestyle when they no longer have children to tell them what to do."

# 36.
# The Apostle Raises Pigeons

Anonymous

According to tradition, when the apostle John was bishop in Ephesus, his hobby was raising pigeons. On one occasion a local official passed John's house on his return from a hunting trip. When he saw John playing with one of the pigeons, the official gently chided the aging bishop for spending his time so frivolously. John looked at the bow his critic was carrying and remarked that the string was loosened.

"Yes," said the hunter, "I loosen the string of my bow when it's not in use. If it always stayed taut, it would lose its rebounding power and fail me in a hunt."

"And I," replied John, "am now relaxing the bow of my mind so that I may be better able to shoot the arrows of divine truth."

# 37.
# Why Do I Work?

### Anonymous

When the company founded by Andrew Carnegie was taken over by the U.S. Steel Corporation in 1901, it acquired as one of its obligations a contract to pay the top Carnegie executive, Charles M. Schwab, the unheard of minimum salary of a million dollars.

J. P. Morgan of U.S. Steel was in a quandary about it. The highest salary on record at the time was $100,000. He met with Schwab, showed him the contract and hesitatingly asked what could be done about it.

"This," said Schwab, as he took the contract and tore it up. That contract had paid Schwab $1,300,000 the previous year.

Schwab later told a *Forbes* interviewer, "I didn't care what salary they paid me. I was not animated by money motives. I believed in what I was trying to do and I wanted to see it brought about. I canceled that contract without a moment's hesitation.

"Why do I work? I work for just the pleasure I find in work, the satisfaction there is in developing things, in creating. Also, the associations business begets. The person who does not work for the love of work, but only for money, is not likely to make money nor to find much fun in life."


# 38.
# A Handful of Pebbles

### Anonymous

A man was walking out in the desert when a voice said to him, "Pick up some pebbles; put them in your pocket, and tomorrow you will be both sorry and glad."

33

The man obeyed. He stooped down and picked up a handful of pebbles and put them in his pocket. The next morning he reached into his pocket and found diamonds, rubies and emeralds. He was both glad and sorry. Glad that he had picked up some pebbles, and sorry that he hadn't picked up more.

And so too it is with the Word of God.

# 39.
# Bible Study Questions

### John De Vries

When you read a passage from Scripture, reflect on its meaning; then ask yourself these questions:

- What did you like about the passage?

- What did you not like?

- What did you not understand?

- What did you learn about God?

- What will you do with what you have read?

- What phrase can you take with you today?

# 40.
# A Parable of Church Workers

### Anonymous

Fred Somebody, Thomas Everybody, Peter Anybody and Joe Nobody were neighbors, but they were not like you,

I'm sure. They were odd people and most difficult to understand. The way they lived was a shame.

All four belonged to the same church, but you would not have enjoyed worshiping with them. Everybody went fishing on Sunday or stayed home to visit with friends. Anybody wanted to worship but was afraid Somebody wouldn't speak to him. So guess who went to church? Yep—Nobody.

Really, Nobody was the only decent one of the lot. Nobody did parish visitations. Nobody worked on the church's committees.

Once they needed a Sunday school teacher. Everybody thought Anybody would do it, while Anybody thought Somebody would do it. And you know who actually did apply for the position? That's right—Nobody!

# 41.
## Hiding behind Masks

### Anonymous

A man came back from a weekend retreat experience, and when a neighbor asked him how it had gone, he said, "I died!"

Puzzled, the neighbor asked him what he meant. "You see," the man answered, "I went to this thing not knowing what to expect. But in the process of that long weekend, I discovered that I had spent my whole life hiding behind a lot of masks. I realized that I had never even let my wife see me as I really was. I'd been playing games with her, playing games with my children, and playing games with others—never letting anybody know who I really am. The worst of it was to discover that even I didn't know myself. I was not in touch with my own honest feelings about myself. And, as all this was being exposed over the weekend, I died over and over again."

He went on, "It is a painful thing for a middle-aged man to discover that he is not even in touch with his own honest

35

feelings about himself. I am convinced," he said, "that I had to go through this death experience in order to become the new person that I hope to be now."

As Scripture says, "Unless a grain of wheat falls to earth and dies, it remains just a grain of wheat; but if it dies, it bears much fruit" (John 12:24).

# 42.
# The Tale of Three Trees

## Traditional Folktale

Long ago, high on a mountaintop, three little trees were talking about their dreams for their future.

The first little tree said, "I'd really like to be made into a cradle so that a newborn baby could rest comfortably and I could support that new life."

The second little tree looked down at a small stream that was flowing into a big river and said, "I'd like to be made into a great ship and be able to carry useful cargo all over the world."

The third little tree viewed the valley from its mountaintop and said, "I don't want to be made into anything. I just want to remain here and grow so tall that I remind people to raise their eyes and think of the God in heaven who loves them."

Years passed and the little trees grew tall and mighty. Then one day, three woodcutters climbed the mountain to begin the harvest of the trees.

As they cut down the first tree, one of them said, "We'll make this one into a manger." The tree shook its branches in protest—it didn't want to become a feed box for animals. It had grander thoughts of beauty. But the woodcutters made it into a manger and sold it to an innkeeper in a small town called Bethlehem. And when the Lord of all the earth was born, he was placed in that manger. Suddenly, the first tree realized it was cradling the greatest treasure in the world.

As the woodcutters cut down the second tree, they said,

"We'll make this one into a fishing boat," and a man named Simon Peter bought it. And when the Lord of all the earth needed a place from which to address the crowds that were pressing in upon him, he got into the little fishing boat to proclaim the Good News. And suddenly the second tree knew he was carrying a most precious cargo—the King of heaven and earth.

Then the woodcutters came to the third tree and said, "The Romans are paying good money these days for wooden beams for their crosses. We'll cut this tree into beams for a cross." The tree protested so hard that its leaves began to fall to the ground, but it was cut down and made into beams.

One Friday morning, the third tree was startled when its beams were taken from a woodpile and shoved onto the shoulders of a man. The tree flinched when soldiers nailed the man's hands to the wood; the tree felt shamed and humiliated.

But early on Sunday, as the dawn appeared, the earth trembled with joy beneath the tree. The tree knew that the Lord of all the earth had been crucified on its cross, but now God's love had changed everything. And the cross from that third tree still stands tall to remind people to raise their eyes and think of the God in heaven who loves them.

And did you notice, in this simple story, how in each case, being cut down was the price they paid for entering into God's glory?

# 43.
# What's under Your Feet?

Anonymous

One day in the hot Arizona desert, when a lonely miner's burro ran off, he thought the world had come to an end. In a fit of anger, he reached down and picked up a rock to hurl after the fool animal. Feeling the weight of the rock, he knew he'd found gold and struck it rich.

The miner found what turned out to be one of the richest gold mines in what was then the Arizona Territory. Would he have found the gold if the burro had not run off? Maybe, and then, maybe not.

# 44.
## Catholics Just Don't Get Excited

Emeric A. Lawrence, O.S.B.

A young Baptist woman, while taking a course in Catholic theology, recorded in her journal her reactions to the Easter vigil service she attended with a few other students.

"I went to Mass tonight. I am not a Catholic, but I was really wanting to join in fellowship and to praise God, so I went. I thought that, since it was Easter time, it would be an exciting Mass, with exciting people. But I sat and kept waiting for the excitement that never came. Even the priest wasn't excited. He read the prayers. That was hard to believe; I mean, wow! Couldn't he come up with a praising and rejoicing prayer from his own heart? And the people surely were not excited—they rushed through everything just to get it done, then rushed out of church. Even communion was rushed and seemed to be listless.

"Come on, people! Jesus is alive! He died and rose again. So can we too. I think that's exciting! I don't know what it is, but the people at Mass tonight seemed to have missed the whole thing. I saw people who have heard the Good News, some of whom I myself have talked to about Jesus and eternal life. I can see now why they think religion is a bore. The Catholic people just are not excited. If the priest was, it wasn't passed on to the people. I just pray that they will open up to the Holy Spirit and God. Liturgy and devotions may not be all that exciting to you, but life in Jesus Christ is more exciting than anything. I know and I praise God for that."

# 45.
## Love Produces Miracles

Anonymous

Some time ago there was a story about a baby boy in a Milwaukee hospital. The baby was born blind and mentally retarded and had cerebral palsy. He was little more than a vegetable and didn't respond to sound or touch. His parents had abandoned him.

The hospital didn't know what to do with the child. Then someone mentioned May Lempke, a nurse who lived nearby. She had already raised five children of her own. May was asked to take the infant, being told, "He'll probably die young."

May responded, "If I take the baby, he won't die young, and I'll be happy to take him."

May named the baby Les. It wasn't easy to care for him. Every day she massaged the baby's entire body. She prayed over him; cried over him. A neighbor told her, "You're wasting your life."

Years passed—five, ten, fifteen. It wasn't until Les was sixteen years old that May was able to teach him to stand alone. All this time he never responded to her. But all this time May continued to love him and to pray over him. Then one day May noticed Les's finger plucking a taut string on a package. She wondered if it was possible that Les was sensitive to music?

May surrounded Les with music. She played every type of music imaginable, hoping that one might appeal to him. Eventually May and her husband bought a second-hand piano and put it in Les's room. May took his fingers and showed him how to push the keys down, but Les didn't appear to understand.

Then one winter night May awoke to the sound of someone playing Tchaikovsky's *Piano Concerto No.1*. What May and her husband discovered was beyond their wildest dreams. Les was sitting at the piano smiling and playing the piece by ear. It was too remarkable to be true. Les had never gotten out of bed alone before. He'd never seated himself at the piano before. He'd never even struck a key on his own. Now Les was playing beautifully.

May dropped to her knees and said, "Thank you, God. You didn't forget Les."

Soon Les began to live at the piano. He played classical, country, ragtime, gospel and even rock. It was absolutely incredible. All the music that May had played for him was stored in Les's brain and was now flowing out through his hands into the piano.

Les, when he was twenty-eight, began to talk. He didn't carry on extended conversations; but he did ask questions, give simple answers and make brief comments.

Les now plays concerts for church groups, civic groups, hospitals, support groups. He even appeared on national television.

Doctors describe Les as an autistic savant, a person who is brain damaged, but extremely talented. They can't explain this unusual phenomenon, although doctors have known about it for nearly two hundred years.

May Lempke can't explain it either. But she does know how the talent can be released—through compassionate love.

## 46.
## The Power of the Saw

Anonymous

Every Saturday morning seems to be the time to check out the latest fix-up list posted on the household refrigerator door, which usually leads to a trip to the local hardware store. Once a do-it-yourselfer went into a hardware store and asked about a new saw for cutting firewood. The salesman took a chain saw from the shelf and told him it was the newest model, with the latest in technology, guaranteed to cut ten cords of wood a day. The customer thought that sounded great, so he bought it on the spot.

The next day the customer returned, looking somewhat exhausted. "Something must be wrong with this saw," he moaned. "I worked as hard as I could and only managed to cut five cords of firewood. I used to cut seven with my old saw."

Confused, the salesman said, "Here, let me try it out back on some wood we keep there." They went to the wood-pile, the salesman pulled the starter cord, and as the motor went *Vvrrooomm,* the customer jumped back shouting, "What's that noise?"

The customer trying to saw wood without the power of the saw to help him is very much like the believer who attempts to live the Christian life without the daily empowerment of the Holy Spirit.

# 47.
# Power of Questions

### Anonymous

Isidore Robey, a famous physicist, came to the United States as a small child and grew up on New York City's Lower East Side. In an interview he once was asked how a poor immigrant boy was able to become one of the world's leading physicists.

He replied, "I couldn't help it. It was because of my mother. She had a deep appreciation for the search for the truth. And every single day when I came home from school, she would ask me, 'Did you ask any good questions today?'"

## 48.
## Kindness Is Stronger

### Dr. Norman Vincent Peale

Doctor Norman Vincent Peale recounts a story his father told him about a reporter he knew who covered William McKinley's campaign for the presidency of the United States. His newspaper was violently opposed to McKinley, and he was supposed to travel on the train with McKinley and send back negative stories at every opportunity.

At first he did—and McKinley knew it. But one bitterly cold afternoon the reporter fell asleep, huddled on the green plush end of the unheated railroad car. McKinley came by, stopped and spread his own overcoat over the man.

When the reporter awoke and found out what had occurred, he resigned from the paper. He could no longer malign a man big enough to answer his criticisms with kindness.

## 49.
## The Grain of Rice

### Anonymous

Once there was a good king who ruled wisely and who ruled well. He was loved by all the people of his kingdom. One day the king called his four daughters together and told them that he was leaving on a long journey. "I wish to learn more about God. I am going to a far off monastery to spend a long time in prayer. In my absence I am leaving the four of you in charge of my kingdom."

"Oh, Father," they cried, "don't leave us. We will never be able to rule the kingdom without you."

The king smiled. "You'll do well in my absence," he said. "Now before I leave, I wish to give each of you a gift. It is my prayer that this gift will help you learn how to rule." The king placed a single grain of rice in each daughter's hand. Then he left on his journey.

The oldest daughter immediately went to her room. She tied a long golden thread around the grain of rice and placed it in a beautiful crystal box. Every day she picked up the box and looked at it.

The second daughter also went to her room, where she placed the grain of rice in a wooden box and put it in a secure spot—under her bed.

The third daughter, a very pragmatic young woman, looked at the grain of rice and thought, "This grain of rice is no different from any other grain of rice." She simply threw the grain of rice away.

The youngest daughter took her grain of rice to her room and wondered about the significance of the gift. She wondered for a week, then a month. When nearly a year passed, she understood the meaning of the gift.

Months turned into years, and the four daughters ruled their father's kingdom. And then one day, the king returned. His beard was full and his eyes sparkled with illumination gained through years of prayer. The king greeted each of his daughters, then asked to see the gifts he had left with them.

The oldest daughter rushed to her room and brought back the crystal box. "Father," she began, "I carefully tied a golden thread around the grain of rice and have kept it near my bed where I have looked at it every day since you left."

Bowing to his daughter, the king accepted the box and said, "Thank you."

Next, the second daughter presented her father with a wooden box containing the grain of rice. "All these years I've kept the rice secure under my bed," she said. "Here it is."

Again the father bowed to his daughter, accepted the box, and said, "Thank you."

The third daughter rushed into the kitchen, found a grain of rice, ran back and said, "Father, here is my grain of rice."

Smiling, the king accepted the grain of rice, bowed, and said, "Thank you."

Finally the youngest daughter stepped before her father and said, "I do not have the grain of rice that you gave me," she said.

"Well, what have you done with it?" the king inquired.

"Father, I thought about that grain of rice for nearly a year before I discovered the meaning of the gift. I realized that the grain of rice was a seed. So I planted it in the ground. Soon it grew, and from it I harvested other seeds. I then planted all those seeds, and again I harvested the crop. Father, I've continued to do this. Come outside, look at the results."

The king followed his daughter where he looked out at an enormous crop of rice stretching as far as the eye could see. There was enough rice to feed the entire nation.

Stepping before his daughter, the king took off his golden crown and placed it on her head. "You have learned the meaning of how to rule," he said softly.

From that day on, the youngest daughter ruled the kingdom. She ruled long, wisely and well.


## 50.
## Lessons from the *Titanic*

Anonymous

In its day, the *Titanic* was the world's largest ship, weighing 46,328 tons. It was $882\frac{1}{2}$ feet long and had three anchors weighing more than ten tons each. It employed a crew of 400 and a hotel staff of 518, and could carry 2,433 passengers. The 159 furnaces burned 650 tons of coal a day. The ship had a complete gymnasium, heated pool, squash court and the first miniature golf course—all below deck. Its lavish appointments included opulent dining rooms with twenty-four-hour service, palm courts and gilded Turkish baths. A number of men and women from the society pages were on the passenger list.

Late during the night of April 14-15, 1912, the "unthinkable" happened to the "unsinkable." Near midnight, the great *Titanic* struck an iceberg, ripping a three-hundred-foot hole through five of its sixteen watertight compartments. It sank in two and one-half hours killing 1,513 people.

Before the unsinkable *Titanic* sank, warning after warning had been sent to tell the crew that they were speeding into an ice field, but the messages were ignored. In fact, when a nearby ship sent an urgent warning, the *Titanic* was talking to Cape Race about the time chauffeurs were to meet arriving passengers at the dock in New York, and what dinner menus were to be ready.

Preoccupied with trivia, the *Titanic* responded to the warning, "Shut up. I am talking to Cape Race. You are jamming my signals."

Why did so many die? The crew disregarded the possible danger of the weather; there were not enough lifeboats on board; and the radio operator of the nearby *California* was off duty.

Question: Will Jesus return on the day of judgment and the "unthinkable" happen to you because you failed to heed warning after warning? What good "reasons" (excuses) will you have? When will you stop being a stubborn and stiff-necked people?

# 51.
# A Kind Word

## Scott Adams

What is the value of a kind word?

In January of 1986 I was flipping through the channels on TV and saw the closing credits for a PBS show called

"Funny Business," a program about cartooning. I had always wanted to be a cartoonist but never knew how to go about it. I wrote to the host of the show, cartoonist Jack Cassady, and asked his advice on entering the profession.

A few weeks later I got an encouraging handwritten letter from Jack, answering all of my specific questions about materials and process. He went on to warn me about the likelihood of being rejected at first, advising me not to get discouraged if that happened. He said the cartoon samples I had sent him were good and worthy of publication.

I got very excited, finally understanding how the whole process worked. I submitted my best cartoons to *Playboy* and the *New Yorker.* The magazines quickly rejected me with cold, little, photocopied form letters. Discouraged, I put my art supplies in the closet and decided to forget about cartooning.

In June of 1987—out of the blue—I got a second letter from Jack Cassady. This was surprising, since I hadn't even thanked him for the original advice. Here's what his letter said:

*Dear Scott,*

*I was reviewing my "Funny Business" mail file when I again ran across your letter and copies of your cartoons. I remember answering your letter.*

*The reason I'm dropping you this note is to again encourage you to submit your ideas to various publications. I hope you have already done so and are on the road to making a few bucks and having some fun too.*

*Sometimes encouragement in the funny business of graphic humor is hard to come by. That's why I am encouraging you to hang in there and keep drawing.*

*I wish you lots of luck, sales and good drawing.*
*Sincerely,*
*Jack*

I was profoundly touched by his letter, largely I think because Jack had nothing to gain—including my thanks, if history was any indication. I acted on his encouragement, dragged my art supplies out of storage and inked the sample strips that eventually became *Dilbert*. Now, seven hundred newspapers and six books later, things are going pretty well in Dilbertville.

I feel certain that I wouldn't have tried cartooning again if Jack hadn't sent the second letter. With a kind word and a postage stamp, he started a chain of events that reaches all the way to you right now. As *Dilbert* became more successful I came to appreciate the enormity of Jack's simple act of kindness. I did eventually thank him, but I could never shake the feeling that I had been given a gift which defied reciprocation. Somehow, "thanks" didn't seem to be enough.

Over time I have come to understand that some gifts are meant to be passed on, not repaid.

I expect at least a million people to read this newsletter. Each of you knows somebody who would benefit from a kind word. I'm encouraging you to act on it before the end of the year. For the biggest impact, do it in writing. And do it for somebody who knows you have nothing to gain.

It's important to give encouragement to family and friends, but their happiness and yours are inseparable. For the maximum velocity, I'm suggesting that you give your encouragement to someone who can't return the favor—it's a distinction that won't be lost on the recipient.

And remember, there's no such thing as a small act of kindness. Every act creates a ripple with no logical end.

# 52.
# The Wemmick

Anonymous

Here's something to reflect on....

The Wemmicks were small, wooden people. Each of the wooden people was carved by a woodworker named Eli. His workshop sat on a hill overlooking their village.

Every Wemmick was different. Some had big noses; others had large eyes. Some were tall and others were short. Some wore hats; others wore coats. But all were made by the same carver and all lived in the village.

And all day, every day, the Wemmicks did the same thing: they gave each other stickers. Each Wemmick had a box of golden star stickers and a box of gray dot stickers. Up and down the streets all over the city, people could be seen sticking stars or dots on one another.

The pretty ones, those with smooth wood and fine paint, always got stars. But if the wood was rough or the paint chipped, the Wemmicks gave dots.

The talented ones got stars too. Some could lift big sticks high above their heads or jump over tall boxes. Still others knew big words or could sing very pretty songs. Everyone gave them stars.

Some Wemmicks had stars all over them! Every time they got a star it made them feel so good that they did something else and got another star.

Others, though, could do little. They got dots.

Punchinello was one of these. He tried to jump high like the others, but he always fell. And when he fell, the others would gather around and give him dots.

Sometimes when he fell, it would scar his wood, so the people would give him more dots.

He would try to explain why he fell by telling something silly, and the Wemmicks would give him more dots.

After a while he had so many dots that he didn't want to go outside. He was afraid he would do something dumb such as forget his hat or step in the water, and then people would give him another dot. In fact, he had so many gray dots that some people would come up and give him one without reason.

"He deserves lots of dots," the wooden people would agree with one another. "He's not a good wooden person."

After a while Punchinello believed them. "I'm not a good Wemmick," he would say.

The few times he went outside, he hung around other Wemmicks who had a lot of dots. He felt better around them.

One day he met a Wemmick who was unlike any he'd ever met. She had no dots or stars. She was just wooden. Her name was Lucia.

It wasn't that people didn't try to give her stickers; it's just that the stickers didn't stick. Some admired Lucia for having no dots, so they would run up and give her a star. But it would fall off. Some would look down on her for having no stars, so they would give her a dot. But it wouldn't stay either.

"That's the way I want to be," thought Punchinello. "I don't want anyone's marks." So he asked the stickerless Wemmick how she did it.

"It's easy," Lucia replied. "Every day I go see Eli."

"Eli?"

"Yes, Eli, the woodcarver. I sit in the workshop with him."

"Why?"

"Why don't you find out for yourself? Go up the hill. He's there." And with that the Wemmick with no marks turned and skipped away.

"But he won't want to see me!" Punchinello cried out. Lucia didn't hear. So Punchinello went home. He sat near a window and watched the wooden people as they scurried around giving each other stars and dots. "It's not right," he muttered to himself. And he resolved to go see Eli.

He walked up the narrow path to the top of the hill and stepped into the big shop. His wooden eyes widened at the size of everything. The stool was as tall as he was. He had to stretch on his tiptoes to see the top of the workbench. A hammer was as long as his arm. Punchinello swallowed hard. "I'm not staying here!" and he turned to leave.

Then he heard his name.

"Punchinello?" The voice was deep and strong.

Punchinello stopped.

"Punchinello! How good to see you. Come and let me have a look at you."

Punchinello turned slowly and looked at the large bearded craftsman. "You know my name?" the little Wemmick asked.

"Of course I do. I made you."

Eli stooped down and picked him up and set him on the bench. "Hmm," the maker spoke thoughtfully as he inspected the gray circles. "Looks like you've been given some bad marks."

"I didn't mean to, Eli. I really tried hard."

"Oh, you don't have to defend yourself to me, child. I don't care what the other Wemmicks think."

"You don't?"

"No, and you shouldn't either. Who are they to give stars or dots? They're Wemmicks just like you. What they think doesn't matter, Punchinello. All that matters is what I think. And I think you are pretty special."

Punchinello laughed. "Me, special? Why? I can't walk fast. I can't jump. My paint is peeling. Why do I matter to you?"

Eli looked at Punchinello, put his hands on those small wooden shoulders, and spoke very slowly. "Because you're mine. That's why you matter to me."

Punchinello had never had anyone look at him like this—much less his maker. He didn't know what to say.

"Every day I've been hoping you'd come," Eli explained.

"I came because I met someone who had no marks."

"I know. She told me about you."

"Why don't the stickers stay on her?"

"Because she has decided that what I think is more important than what they think. The stickers only stick if you let them."

"What?"

"The stickers only stick if they matter to you. The more you trust my love, the less you care about the stickers."

"I'm not sure I understand."

"You will, but it will take time. You've got a lot of

marks. For now, just come to see me every day and let me remind you how much I care."

Eli lifted Punchinello off the bench and set him on the ground.

"Remember," Eli said as the Wemmick walked out the door, "you are special because I made you. And I don't make mistakes."

Punchinello didn't stop, but in his heart he thought, "I think he really means it."

With that thought in his mind, a dot fell to the ground.

# 53.
## To Teach in Parables and Stories

Anthony de Mello, S.J.

The master taught mostly in parables and stories. One day, someone asked one of his disciples where he got them from.

"Mostly from God," said the disciple. "When God means for you to be a healer, he sends you patients; when he makes you a teacher, God sends you students; when he destines you to be a master, he sends you stories."

# 54.
## Face the Music

Anonymous

The expression "face the music" is said to have originated in China. According to the story, one man in the court orchestra could not play a note. Being a person of great influence and wealth, he demanded that he be given a place in the group because he wanted to perform before the prince. The conductor agreed to let him sit in the back row of the orchestra, even though he couldn't read the music. He was given a flute, and when the other flutists raised their instruments, he'd raise his flute, pucker his lips and move his fingers. He would go through the motions of playing, but never make a sound. This deception continued for several years.

Then a new conductor took over. He told the orchestra that he wanted to audition each player individually. One by one they performed in his presence. Then came the flutist's turn. He was frantic with worry, so he pretended to be sick. A doctor was summoned to examine him and declared him to be perfectly well. The conductor then insisted the man appear and demonstrate his skill. Shamefacedly he confessed that he was a fake. He was unable to "face the music."

# 55.
# Where Have All the Sermons Gone?

Anonymous

When a preacher died, it was discovered that he had tied together copies of all his sermons and placed a card on top of them with this inscription: "Where has the influence gone of all these sermons I've preached?"

Underneath, he had scribbled in large letters—**"OVER."**

On the other side this answer was found: "Where are last year's sunrays? They have gone into fruits and grain and vegetables to feed people. Where are last year's raindrops? Forgotten by most people, of course, but they did their refreshing work, and their influence still abides. So, too, my sermons have gone into people's lives and made them nobler, more Christ-like, and better fitted for heaven."

## 56.
## Love: Creamy or Crunchy?

Kathy Noller

A mother relates this story: "As our children entered college, my husband and I found we were not financially prepared. As a result, almost every dime we made went for tuition, housing and other college expenses. Our children's part-time jobs covered very little. We went without food, decent clothing and necessities on a regular basis. I prayed a lot, believe me.

"One day I mentioned my craving for peanut butter to my husband. We laughed—no coupons, no peanut butter. A few days later, when he went to work, I wondered what I would prepare for supper. Out of habit, though I knew the shelves were bare, I looked in the fridge, then in the cupboards.

"There, in the middle of the shelf was a jar of peanut butter. I can't really tell you what came over me; holding that jar, I felt love, warmth, hope. Who would ever think peanut butter could do so much!

"Some husbands bring home flowers. Mine brought a jar of peanut butter. Actually, I prefer to call it love."


## 57.
## Are You Going to Help Me?

Mark V. Hansen

In 1989 an 8.2 earthquake almost flattened Armenia, killing over thirty thousand people in less than four minutes. In the midst of utter devastation and chaos, a father left his wife securely at home and rushed to the school where his son was supposed to be, only to discover that the building was as flat as a pancake.

After the traumatic initial shock, he remembered the

promise he had made to his son. "No matter what, I'll always be there for you!" Tears began to fill his eyes. As he looked at the pile of debris that once was the school, it looked hopeless, but he kept remembering his commitment to his son.

He began to concentrate on where he walked his son to class at school each morning. Remembering that his son's classroom would be in the back right corner of the building, he rushed there and started digging through the rubble.

As he was digging, other forlorn parents arrived, clutching their hearts, saying: "My son!" "My daughter!" Other well-meaning parents tried to pull him off of what was left of the school saying, "It's too late!"

"They're dead!"

"You can't help!"

"Go home!"

"Come on, face reality. There's nothing you can do!"

"You're just going to make things worse!"

To each parent he responded with one line, "Are you going to help me now?" And then he proceeded to dig for his son, stone by stone.

The fire chief showed up and tried to pull him off of the school's debris saying, "Fires are breaking out, explosions are happening everywhere. You're in danger. We'll take care of it. Go home." To which this loving, caring Armenian father asked, "Are you going to help me now?"

The police came and said, "You're angry and distraught. It's over. You're endangering others. Go home. We'll handle it!" To which the father replied, "Are you going to help me now?" No one helped.

Courageously, he proceeded alone because he needed to know for himself. "Is my boy alive or is he dead?" he asked. He dug for eight hours...twelve hours...twenty-four hours...thirty-six hours...then, in the thirty-eighth hour, he pulled back a boulder and heard his son's voice. He screamed his son's name, "ARMAND!" He heard back, "Dad!?! It's me, Dad! I told the other kids not to worry. I told 'em that if you were alive, you'd save me, and when you saved me, they'd be saved. You promised, 'No matter what, I'll always be there for you!' You did it, Dad!"

"What's going on in there? How is it?" the father asked.

"There are fourteen of us left out of thirty-three, Dad. We're scared, hungry, thirsty and thankful you're here. When the building collapsed, it made a wedge, like a triangle, and it saved us."

"Come on out, boy!"

"No, Dad! Let the other kids out first, 'cause I know you'll get me! No matter what, I know you'll be there for me."

# 58.
# If a Child Lives with...

Anonymous

If a child lives with criticism, she learns to condemn.
If a child lives with hostility, he learns to fight.
If a child lives with fears, she learns to be apprehensive.
If a child lives with pity, he learns to feel sorry for himself.
If a child lives with jealousy, she learns to feel guilty.
If a child lives with encouragement, he learns to be confident.
If a child lives with tolerance, she learns to be patient.
If a child lives with praise, he learns to be appreciative.
If a child lives with acceptance, she learns to love.
If a child lives with approval, he learns to like himself.
If a child lives with recognition, she learns to have a goal.
If a child lives with fairness, he learns what justice is.
If a child lives with honesty, she learns what truth is.
If a child lives with security, he learns to have faith in himself and in those about him.
If a child lives with friendliness, she learns that the world is a good place in which to live.

## 59.
# Ten Commandments of Sports for Parents

Anonymous

1. Thou shall be sure that your child knows that—win or lose, scared or heroic—you love him, appreciate his efforts, and that you are not disappointed in him.

2. Thou shall try your best to be completely honest about your child's athletic capability, her competitive attitude, her sportsmanship—and her **actual** skill level.

3. Thou shall be helpful, but don't coach him on the way to the rink, track, court, field or pool, or on the way back home.

4. Thou shall teach your child to enjoy competition for competition's sake, remembering that there are lessons to be learned in winning as well as in losing.

5. Hearken, O parents: try not to relive your athletic life through your child—or try to create an athletic career to replace the one that you never had.

6. Thou shall not compete with the coach. Remember, in many cases, the coach becomes a hero to the athletes—a person who can do no wrong.

7. Thou shall not compare the skill, courage or attitudes of your child with those of other members of the squad or team—at least not within his hearing.

8. Thou shall get to know the coach so that you can be sure that her philosophy, attitudes, ethics and knowledge are such that you are happy to expose your child to her.

9. Always remember that children tend to exaggerate, both when praised and when criticized. Temper your reactions when they bring home tales of woe—or tales of heroics.

10. Thou shall make a point of understanding courage and the fact that it is relative. Some of us climb mountains but fear flight—some of us will want to fight, but turn to jelly if a spider crawls nearby. A child must learn: **Courage is not absence of fear, but rather doing something in spite of fear.**

# 60.
## The Otter's Children

### Jewish Folktale

The Otter rushed before the king crying aloud, "My lord, you are a king who loves justice and rules fairly. You have established peace among all your creatures, and yet there is no peace."

"Who has broken the peace?" demanded the king.

"The Weasel!" shouted the Otter. "I dove into the water to hunt for food for my children, leaving them in the care of the Weasel. While I was gone, my children were killed. 'An eye for an eye,' the Good Book says. I demand vengeance!"

The king sent for the Weasel, who soon appeared before him.

"You have been charged with the death of the Otter's children. How do you plead?" demanded the king.

"Alas, my lord," wept the Weasel, "I am responsible for the death of the Otter's children, though it was clearly an accident. As I heard the Woodpecker sound the danger alarm, I rushed to defend our land. In doing so I trampled the Otter's children by accident."

The king summoned the Woodpecker. "Is it true that you sounded the alarm with your mighty beak?" inquired the king.

"It is true, my lord," replied the Woodpecker. "I began the alarm when I spied the Scorpion sharpening its dagger."

When the Scorpion appeared before the king, it was asked if it indeed had sharpened its dagger. "You understand that sharpening your dagger is an act of war?" declared the king.

"I understand," replied the Scorpion, "but I prepared only because I observed the Turtle polishing its armor."

In its defense the Turtle said, "I would not have polished my armor had not I seen the Crab preparing its sword."

The Crab declared, "I saw the Lobster swinging its javelin."

When the Lobster appeared before the king, it explained, "I began to swing my javelin when I saw the Otter swimming toward my children, ready to devour them."

Turning to the Otter, the king announced, "You, not the Weasel, are the guilty party. The blood of your children is upon your head. Whoever sows death, shall reap it."

# 61.
# Sunday School's Easter Lesson

### Ben Haden

A group of four-year-olds were gathered in a Sunday school class in Chattanooga. The teacher looked at the class and asked this question: "Does anyone know what today is?"

A little four-year-old girl held up her hand and said, "Yes, today is Palm Sunday." The teacher exclaimed, "That's fantastic, that's wonderful! Now does anyone know what next Sunday is?"

The same little girl held up her hand and said, "Yes, next Sunday is Easter Sunday."

Once again the teacher said, "That's fantastic. Now, does anyone know what makes next Sunday Easter?"

The same little girl responded and said, "Yes, next

Sunday is Easter because Jesus rose from the grave," and before the teacher could congratulate her, she kept on talking and said, "but if he sees his shadow he has to go back in for six weeks."

# 62.
# A Giving Tree

Anonymous

There is an old tale about an unusual tree that grew outside the gates of a desert city. It was an ancient tree, a landmark, as a matter of fact. It seemed to have been touched by the finger of God, for it bore fruit perpetually. Despite its old age, its limbs were constantly laden with fruit. Hundreds of passersby refreshed themselves from the tree, as it never failed to give freely of its fruit.

But then a greedy merchant purchased the property on which the tree grew. He saw hundreds of travelers picking the fruit from *his* tree, so he built a high fence around it. Travelers pleaded and pleaded with the new owner, "Share the fruit with us."

The miserly merchant scoffed, "It's my tree, my fruit, and bought with my money."

And then an astonishing thing happened—suddenly, the ancient tree died! What could have happened? The law of giving, as predictable as the law of gravity, expresses the immutable principle: when giving stops, bearing fruit ceases, and death follows inevitably.

# 63.
# The Chief's Three Sons

Anonymous

Once there was a Native American chief who was nearing the end of his life. Even though he had tried many times, he was not able to decide which of his sons should succeed as chief.

One day he gathered his sons together and told them, "Do you see that mountain in the distance? I want you to journey to that mountain, climb to its summit and bring back the thing you think will be most helpful in leading our people."

After several days the first son returned with a load of flint stones, used to make arrow tips and spear points. He told his father, "Our people will never live in fear of their enemies. I know where there is a mound of flint."

The second son climbed to the top of the mountain, and on the way found forests rich with wood for making fires. When he returned he said to his father, "Our people will never be cold in winter. I know where wood can be found in abundance to keep them warm and to cook their food."

The third son returned late and empty-handed. He stated, "When I got to the summit I found nothing worth bringing back. I searched everywhere, but the top of the mountain was barren rock and useless. Then I looked out toward the horizon, far into the distance. I was astonished to see new land filled with forests and meadows, mountains and valleys, fish and animals—a land of great beauty and great peace. I brought nothing back, for the land was still far off and I didn't have time to travel there. But I would love to go there someday; I delayed coming back because I found it very difficult to return after seeing the beauty of that land."

The old chief's eyes blazed. He grasped this third son in his arms proclaiming that he would succeed him as the new chief. He thought to himself, "The other sons brought back worthy things, necessary things. But my third son knows the way to a better land. It is important that the new chief has a vision and has seen the promised land and burns with the desire to go there."

# 64.
# A Warm Preaching

Anonymous

After he had spoken during a preaching mission for parish renewal, a renowned evangelist said that a young woman came up to thank him for restoring her faith, and told him that he was a very warm preacher.

Later that evening, as he reflected over the event, he was complimenting himself, recalling the person's remarks. But, then, he remembered that in the dictionary the definition of warm is not so hot.

# 65.
# Hold My Hand, Father

Anonymous

There is a story about Charlie, who sat by the hospital bed of his young son, just out from major emergency surgery. Dreadful thoughts kept creeping into his mind. Why had he not called the doctor sooner? Why had he not suspected that his son's troubles were more than a stomach ache? Why? Why?

Presently, the youngster stirred, opened his eyes and saw his father sitting nearby. The lad stretched out his small, fevered hand to his father and said, "Hold my hand, Daddy; I hurt so bad."

Charlie took his son's hand; the small boy smiled weakly and drifted off into unconsciousness again. Then Charlie, taking a cue from his son, bowed his head, closed his eyes and whispered, "Hold my hand, Father; I hurt."

## 66.
## Discover Your Potential

Anonymous

A professor of management gave the following assignment to his senior seminar class: "Ask four successful men and women their recommendations to help people unlock their potential."

One student interviewed the CEO of a Fortune 500 company and received this recommendation: "Love your enemies. Do this and you will discover within yourself a potential for loving and forgiving that you never dreamed you had."

## 67.
## What Is the Meaning of Life?
(adapted)

Robert Fulghum

A Greek philosopher and teacher ended a lecture asking, "Are there any questions?" In the audience was Robert Fulghum who asked, "Dr. Papaderos, what is the meaning of life?"

Fulghum relates: "The usual laughter followed, and people stirred to go. Papaderos held up his hand and stilled the room and looked at me for a long time, asking with his eyes if I was serious and seeing from my eyes that I was. 'I will answer your question,' he said. Then taking his wallet out of his hip pocket, he fished into it and brought out a very small, round mirror, about the size of a quarter. Then he said, 'When I was a small child, during the war, we were very poor and we lived in a remote village. One day, on the road, I found several broken pieces of a mirror from a wrecked German motorcycle. I tried to find all the pieces and put them together, but it was not possible, so I kept only the largest piece. *This* one. And by scratching it on a stone I made it round. I began to play with it as a toy and became fascinated by the fact that I could reflect light into dark places where the sun would never shine—in deep holes and crevices and dark closets. It became a game for me to get light into the most inaccessible places I could find. I kept the little mirror, and as I went about my growing up, I would take it out in idle moments and continue the challenge of the game. As I became a man, I grew to understand that this was not just a *child's* game but a metaphor for what I might do with my *life*. I came to understand that I am not the light or the source of light. But light—truth, understanding, knowledge—is there, and it will only shine in many dark places if I *reflect* it.

'I am a fragment of a mirror whose whole design and shape I do not know. Nevertheless, with what I have, I can reflect light into the dark places of this world—into the black places in the hearts of men—and change some things in some people. Perhaps others may see and do likewise. This is what I am *about*. This is the meaning of *my life*.'

"And then he took his small mirror and, holding it carefully, caught the bright rays of daylight streaming through the window and reflected them onto my face and onto my hands folded on the desk."

Where there is darkness, let us bring light;
Where there is despair, let us bring hope;
Let us walk in the Light of the Lord.

# 68.
## Tomorrow

Anonymous

He was going to be all that he wanted to—Tomorrow.
None would be kinder or braver than he—Tomorrow.
A friend who was troubled and weary, he knew,
Who'd be glad of a lift, and who needed it too,
On him he would call and see what he could do—
    Tomorrow.
Each morning he stacked up the letters he'd write—
    Tomorrow.
And thought of the folks he would fill with delight—
    Tomorrow.
But hadn't one minute to stop on his way,
"More time I will give to others," he'd say—Tomorrow.
The greatest of disciples this man would have been—
    Tomorrow.
The world would have hailed him if he had seen—
    Tomorrow.
But, in fact, he passed on, and he faded from view,
And all that he left here when living was through,
Was a mountain of things he intended to do—
    Tomorrow!


# 69.
## He Was a Brick!

Anonymous

Have you ever heard of the expression, "He's a brick!"?
The term implies bravery, courage and loyalty.

Plutarch, in writing about the king of Sparta, tells how
the phrase originated. It seems that an ambassador on a diplo-

matic mission visited the famous city of Sparta. Knowing that its strength was acclaimed throughout all Greece, he expected to see massive fortresses surrounding the city, but he found nothing of the kind. Surprised, the ambassador said to the king, "Sir, you have no fortifications for defense. How can this be?"

"Oh, but we are well protected," replied the king. "Come with me tomorrow and I will show you the walls of Sparta."

The next day he led the ambassador to the plains where Sparta's army was assembled in full battle dress. Pointing proudly to his soldiers, who stood fearlessly in place, the king said, "Behold! The walls of Sparta—ten thousand men and every man a brick!"

# 70.
# The Plastered Crop

### Anonymous

Benjamin Franklin learned that sowing plaster in the fields would make things grow better. He told his neighbors, but they did not believe him. They argued with him, trying to prove that plaster could be of no use at all to grass or grain.

After a little while Franklin let the matter drop and said no more about it. Instead, he went into the field early in the following spring and sowed some grain. Close by the path, where everyone walked, he traced some letters with his finger and applied plaster, mixing it in well with the seeds.

After two weeks, the seeds began to sprout. Ben's neighbors, as they passed, were surprised to see, in a deeper shade of green than the rest of the field, large letters: "This has been plastered."

Ben Franklin did not need to argue with his neighbors any more about the benefit of plaster for the fields. For as the season went on and the grain grew, these bright green letters just rose up above all the rest until they were a kind of relief plate in the field—"This has been plastered."

Bearing fruit is essential to Christian discipleship. A life well lived is a more effective witness than words well said.

# 71.
## God: The Alpha and the Omega

Anonymous

On almost all his musical manuscripts, Johann Sebastian Bach placed two sets of initials. At the beginning he wrote the letters, "J.J."—*Jesu juvet,* "Jesus help me." And at the end he wrote the letters, "S.D.G."—*Soli Deo gloria,* "To God alone be the glory."

Considering that God is to be our beginning and ending, we could do well to inscribe those initials at the beginning and end of each of our days.

# 72.
## Another Way

Terry Dobson

The train clanked and rattled through the suburbs of Tokyo on a drowsy spring afternoon. Our car was comparatively empty—a few housewives with their kids in tow, some old folks going shopping. I gazed absently at the drab houses and dusty hedgerows.

At one station the doors opened, and suddenly the afternoon quiet was shattered by a man bellowing violent, incomprehensible curses. The man staggered into our car. He wore laborer's clothing and was big, drunk and dirty. Screaming, he swung at a woman holding a baby. The blow sent her spinning into the laps of an elderly couple. It was a miracle that the baby was unharmed.

Terrified, the couple jumped up and scrambled toward the other end of the car. The laborer aimed a kick at the retreating back of the old woman, but missed as she scuttled to safety. This so enraged the drunk that he grabbed the metal pole in the center of the car and tried to wrench it out of its stanchion. I could see that one of his hands was cut and bleeding. The train lurched ahead, the passengers frozen with fear. I stood up.

I was young then, some twenty years ago, and in pretty good shape. I'd been putting in a solid eight hours of Aikido training nearly every day for the past three years. I liked to throw and grapple. I thought I was tough. The trouble was, my martial skill was untested in actual combat. As students of Aikido, we were not allowed to fight.

"Aikido," my teacher had said again and again, "is the art of reconciliation. Whoever has the mind to fight has broken his connection with the universe. If you try to dominate people, you're already defeated. We study how to resolve conflict, not how to start it."

I listened to his words. I tried hard. I even went so far as to cross the street to avoid the *chimpira,* the pinball punks who lounged around the train stations. My forbearance exalted me. I felt both tough and holy. In my heart, however, I wanted an absolutely legitimate opportunity whereby I might save the innocent by destroying the guilty.

"This is it!" I said to myself as I got to my feet. "People are in danger. If I don't do something fast, somebody will probably get hurt."

Seeing me stand up, the drunk recognized a chance to focus his rage. "Aha!" he roared. "A foreigner! You need a lesson in Japanese manners!"

I held on lightly to the commuter strap overhead and gave him a slow look of disgust and dismissal. I planned to take this turkey apart, but he had to make the first move. I wanted him mad, so I pursed my lips and blew him an insolent kiss.

"All right!" he hollered. "You're gonna get a lesson!" He gathered himself for a rush at me.

A fraction of a second before he could move, someone shouted, "Hey!" It was earsplitting. I remember the strangely joyous, lilting quality of it—as though you and a friend had been searching diligently for something, and he had suddenly stumbled upon it. "Hey!" I heard it again.

I wheeled to my left; the drunk spun to his right. We both stared down at a little old Japanese man. He must have been well into his seventies, this tiny gentleman, sitting there in his immaculate kimono. He took no notice of me, but beamed delightedly at the laborer, as though he had a most important, most welcome secret to share.

"C'mere," the old man said in an easy vernacular, beckoning to the drunk. "C'mere and talk with me." He waved his hands lightly.

The big man followed, as if on a string. He planted his feet belligerently in front of the old gentleman and roared above the clacking wheels, "Why the hell should I talk to you?" The drunk now had his back to me. If his elbow moved so much as a millimeter, I'd drop him in his socks.

The old man continued to beam at the laborer. "What'cha been drinkin'?" he asked, his eyes sparkling with interest. "I been drinkin' sake," the laborer bellowed back, "and it's none of your business!" Flecks of spittle spattered the old man.

"Oh, that's wonderful," the old man said, "absolutely wonderful! You see, I love sake too. Every night, me and my wife—she's seventy-six, you know—we warm up a little bottle of sake and take it out into the garden, and we sit on an old wooden bench. We watch the sun go down, and we look to see how our persimmon tree is doing. My great grandfather planted that tree, and we worry about whether it will recover from those ice storms we had last winter. Our tree has done better than I expected, though, especially when you consider the poor quality of the soil. It is gratifying to watch when we take our sake and go out to enjoy the evening—even when it rains!" He looked up at the laborer, eyes twinkling.

As he struggled to follow the old man, his face began to soften. His fists slowly unclenched. "Yeah," he said. "I love persimmons too...." His voice trailed off.

"Yes," said the old man, smiling, "and I'm sure you have a wonderful wife."

"No," replied the laborer. "My wife died." Very gently, swaying with the motion of the train, the big man began to sob. "I don't got no wife, I don't got no home, I don't got no job. I'm so ashamed of myself." Tears rolled down his cheeks; a spasm of despair rippled through his body.

As I stood there in my well-scrubbed youthful innocence, my make-this-world-safe-for-democracy righteousness, I felt dirtier than he was.

Then the train arrived at my stop. As the doors opened, I heard the old man cluck sympathetically. "My, my," he said, "that is a difficult predicament indeed. Sit down here and tell me about it."

I turned my head for one last look. The laborer was sprawled on the seat with his head in the old man's lap. The old man was softly stroking the filthy, matted hair.

As the train pulled away, I sat down on a bench in the station. What I had wanted to do with muscle had been accomplished with kind words. I had just seen Aikido in action, and the essence of it was love. I would have to practice the art with an entirely different spirit. It would be a long time before I could speak about the resolution of conflict.

# 73.
# The Woodcutter and the Missionary

## Anonymous

There is a story about a young missionary who spotted a woodcutter at work in a forest. "What a perfect opportunity for me to make a convert for Jesus," he thought when he learned the woodcutter had never heard of Jesus Christ.

All day as the man chopped wood, carried it to his wagon, and walked back to chop another load, the young missionary asked, "Well, are you ready to accept Jesus Christ?"

"I don't know," replied the woodcutter. "All day you spoke to me of this Jesus who helps us with all our burdens, yet you never helped me with mine."

# 74.
# Puppies for Sale

### Anonymous

In a certain city a man put up a sign in his pet store window. The sign read, "Puppies for Sale." Immediately, a small boy entered the store. He asked to see the puppies. The owner whistled and a golden retriever came out from the back room with a trail of puppies scurrying after their mother. A fifth puppy limped behind the others.

The boy spotted the lame puppy and asked, "What's wrong with that one?" The man explained that the puppy was born with a deformed hip. "That pup will live, but it will never be much of a dog," said the man.

The boy replied, "That's the one I want." The man objected, but the boy pulled up his right pant leg revealing a heavy steel brace. The boy said, "I don't run so well myself. The puppy will need somebody who understands."

# 75.
# The Secret of Life

Anonymous

An eight-year-old boy approached an old man in front of a wishing well, looked up into his eyes, and said, "I understand you're a very wise man. I'd like to know the secret of life."

The old man looked down at the youngster and replied, "I've thought a lot in my lifetime, and the secret can be summed up in four words:

"The first is THINK. Think about the values by which you wish to live your life.

"The second is BELIEVE. Believe in yourself based on the thinking you've done about the values by which you're going to live your life.

"The third is DREAM. Dream about the things that can be, based on your belief in yourself and the values by which you're going to live your life.

"The last is DARE. Dare to make your dreams become reality, based on your belief in yourself and your values."

And with that, Walt E. Disney said to the boy, "**Think, Believe, Dream** and **Dare.**"


# 76.
# Sin Is a Sucker

Anonymous

There was a farmer in the Midwest who grew corn the old-fashioned way. When the corn stalks grew to a couple of feet in height, he sent his children into the fields to pull the "suckers" from the stalks. You see, suckers are offshoots from the stalks, angling out from down near the roots, always full of verdant life, but never producing any ears of corn.

The children asked their father why they had to pull those suckers off. His answer: "Those suckers sap the life from the stalk, rob the ears of vital nutrients, take away the stalk's power to grow fully and to produce bountiful corn."

And in our lives sin robs us of the power to grow fully.

# 77.
## Dad, Remember Me

Anonymous

Dan Poling spoke of his last conversation with his son, Clark, before he reported back to the battleship that was to carry him to his death. Clark Poling was one of the four chaplains on the *Dorchester*, an army transport ship, which was sunk on February 3, 1943, during World War II. As their father-son chat came to a close, Clark said, "Dad, remember me as I return to my post of duty."

Dr. Poling replied, "Son, I'll pray every day that God will bring you back home without a scratch."

The young chaplain said, "Dad, please don't pray that way. I want you to pray that I will be adequate for any situation."

When last seen by those who survived this terrible ordeal, Reverend Clark Poling was standing on the deck of the sinking ship, along with the three other chaplains, giving their life jackets to enlisted men. All four chaplains went down with the ship.

# 78.
## A Brother's Sacrifice

Anonymous

Back in the fifteenth century, in a tiny village in Germany, lived a family with eighteen children. Despite a seemingly hopeless situation, two brothers shared a dream to pursue their talent for art. But they knew that the family's financial condition was too tight to pay for their studies.

The two boys came up with their own solution. They would toss a coin. The loser would go into the nearby mines and support his brother attending the art academy. Then that brother, at the end of his studies, would support the other brother at the academy, either with sales of his artwork or, if necessary, also by laboring in the mines.

So one brother went to the art academy while the other went into the dangerous mines. After four years the young artist returned to his village and family. There was a triumphant homecoming dinner. The artist rose from the table to drink a toast to his beloved brother for his years of sacrifice. His closing words were, "And now, Albert, it is your turn. Now you can go to the academy to pursue your dream, and I will support you."

Albert sat there, tears streaming down his face, shaking his lowered head while he sobbed and repeated over and over, "No...no...no!"

Finally, Albert rose and wiped the tears from his eyes. He looked down the long table and, holding his hands out in front of him, he said softly, "No, brother, it is too late for me to go. Look...look at what four years in the mines have done to my hands! The bones in every finger have been crushed at least once, and I've been suffering from arthritis so badly that I cannot hold even a wine glass to return your toast, much less make delicate lines on canvas with a pen or brush. No, brother, for me it is too late."

Then one day, to pay homage to Albert for all that he had sacrificed, Albrecht Dürer painstakingly drew his brother's tortured hands with palms together and crooked fingers pointed skyward. He called his powerful drawing simply *Hands*, but the entire world almost immediately opened their hearts to his masterpiece and renamed his tribute of love *The Praying Hands*.

# 79.
# Desire Begins a Fire

Anonymous

While commenting on the NBA college draft, M. L. Carr, a former Boston Celtics star, said, "They can take a man and measure him, examine him, analyze him and dissect his statistics, but they cannot look into his heart. That's where the thirst is—the hunger. That's where the desire begins a fire."

# 80.
# Your Daily Investment

Anonymous

If you had a bank that credited your account with $86,400, but would not allow you to carry over any balance from one day to the next, what would you do?

Draw out every cent every day, I'd imagine, and use it to your advantage!

Well, you have such a bank, and its name is "Time." Every morning it credits you with 86,400 seconds. Every midnight it rules off as lost whatever of this you failed to invest to good purpose. It carries over no balance. It allows no overdrafts. Each day, it opens a new account with you. Each night, it burns the records of the day. If you fail to use the day's deposits, the loss is yours alone. There is no going back. There is no drawing against tomorrow's account. It is up to each of us to invest wisely this precious fund of hours, minutes and seconds in order to profit from it the utmost in health, happiness and success!

# 81.
## Life Requires a Rhythm

Anonymous

A university biology professor studying horseshoe crabs discovered something very interesting. Their metabolism has a measurable and adaptable rhythm.

Horseshoe crabs live in shallow tidal pools along the Atlantic Ocean. When the tide comes in, they feed. When the tide is out, they rest. As one might expect, their metabolic rates spike at the time of high tide, and they are quiet when the tide ebbs. This metabolic rhythm remains constant even when the crabs are captured and placed in laboratory aquariums.

The professor doing this study moved from the East Coast to Chicago. Naturally, he brought his experimental crustaceans with him. Remarkably, he discovered that the rhythm of life for those horseshoe crabs adjusted to the move. In a matter of a few days, their metabolic rates increased at the precise hour that the tide would reach Chicago—if Chicago had a tide!

The moral: Even crabs have enough sense to recognize that life requires a rhythm and when one's circumstances change, one must adjust. Everyone still needs a time for work and a time for rest.

# 82.
## To Be Remembered for What?
(adapted)

Anonymous

Management expert Peter Drucker recalls a question posed by a teacher when Drucker was thirteen years old. The teacher went right through the class and asked each student, "What do you want to be remembered for?"

None could answer, but the teacher chuckled and said, "I didn't expect you to be able to answer it. But if you still can't answer it by the time you are fifty, then you will have wasted your life."

Drucker went to his sixtieth class reunion, and one of his fellow students asked, "Do you remember Father Pflieger and that question?"

They all remembered it. And each one said it had made a big difference in his life, although each didn't understand it until he was in his forties. They had begun trying to answer the question in their twenties, but the answers they came up with didn't last. It took longer to discover what really mattered.

Drucker went on to say, "I'm always asking that question: What do you want to be remembered for?" He finds that the question induces him to renew himself because it pushes him to see himself as a different person—the person he can *become*.

Drucker believes that people are fortunate if someone with the moral authority of a teacher asks them that question early in their lives; then they will continue to ask it as long as they live.

And you: Will you be remembered? If so, for what? Do you see yourself as capable of being a different person? Who can you yet become in life? Will you speak out with moral authority about character, values, ethics, integrity?

For if you remain silent, what other voices will the children listen to?

## 83.
# The Secret of Success
### (adapted)

Clarence DeLoach, Jr.

A successful businessman once was asked the secret of success. His reply summed up success in three words: AND THEN SOME. He learned early in life that the difference between average people and the truly successful could be simply stated in those three words. Top people did what was expected *and then some!*

Jesus taught the *and then some* principle in the Sermon on the Mount. He is saying: go beyond what is expected! Go a little farther!

Let the words *and then some* serve as a tonic for your spirit. Practice your faith faithfully—*and then some.* Give generously of your time and resources—*and then some.* Greet those you meet with a smile—*and then some.* Meet your obligations; be dependable—*and then some.* Do your best in all things and at all times—*and then some.*

## 84.
## Quality Involves Waiting Patiently

### Anonymous

James Garfield, who later became the twentieth president of the United States, was, in an earlier time, president of Hiram College in Ohio. He once was approached by the father of a young student seeking admission to the college. The father criticized the length and the difficulty of the required curriculum. "Can't you simplify the course work? My son will never get through all this academic work. There should be a shorter route."

Garfield replied, "I believe I can arrange such a plan, but it all depends upon what you want for your son. When God wants to make an oak tree, he takes a hundred years. And, when God wants to make a squash, he requires only two months."

77

# 85.
# The Watchman

### Anonymous

There is an old Hasidic tale about Rabbi Naftali. Now it was the custom of the rich people of his city, whose homes were on the outskirts and sort of isolated, to hire men to watch over their property at night. Thus began the security guard protection business, which is thriving even today.

But back to the tale. Late one evening, as was his custom, Rabbi Naftali was out for a walk, and he met one such watchman walking back and forth. The rabbi asked, "For whom do you work?"

The guard told the rabbi who had hired him, and then the guard inquired, "And for whom do you work, Rabbi?"

The watchman's words struck at the heart of the rabbi, who replied, "I'm not sure whether I work for anyone or not." The rabbi walked along with the watchman for some time in silence. Then he asked, "Will you come and work for me?"

"Oh, Rabbi, I should be honored to be your servant," said the watchman, "but what would be my duties?"

Rabbi Naftali answered quietly, "To keep reminding me with that question."

Like Rabbi Naftali, we need help if we are to remember for whom it is we work. Daily prayer and reading the Bible are our lookouts, our watchmen; they remind us that God is in charge.

# 86.
# Am I Indispensable?

### Anonymous

Walter Damrosch became a full-fledged conductor when he was still in his twenties. Not unexpectedly, the acclaim he received went to his head. He began to think that no one could take his place. Then one day at rehearsal he misplaced his baton.

"Is there an extra baton around?" he asked.

Three violinists immediately produced batons from inside their violin cases. Humbled by this, Damrosch never again regarded himself as indispensable.

## 87.
## What a Fool I've Been!

### Anonymous

There's a story about a tenant farmer who worked hard for many years to improve the production of the land. Then something happened that caused him to become very bitter. When it was time to renew the lease, the owner told him that he was going to sell the farm to his son, who was getting married. The tenant farmer made several generous offers to buy the farm for himself, hoping that the owner's decision would be changed. But it was all in vain.

As the day drew near for the tenant to vacate his home, his weeks of angry brooding finally got the best of him. He gathered seeds from some of the most pesky and noxious weeds he could find. Then he spent many hours scattering them on the fertile soil of the farm, along with a lot of trash and stones.

To his dismay, the very next morning the owner informed him that the plans for his son's wedding fell through; therefore, he'd be happy to renew the tenant's lease. The owner couldn't understand why the tenant exclaimed in such agonizing tones, "Oh, Lord, what a fool I've been!"

# 88.
# The Story of the Oyster

Anonymous

There once was an oyster whose story I tell,
Who found that sand got under its shell;
Just one little grain, but it gave such pain,
For oysters have feelings although they're so plain.
Now, did it berate the workings of Fate
Which had led to such a deplorable state?
Did it curse the government, call for an election
Or cry that the sea should have given protection?
No, as it lay on the ocean shelf, it said to 'self,
"If I cannot remove it, I'll try to improve on it."
So the years rolled by as years always do,
And it came to its ultimate destiny—oyster stew.
Now the small grain of sand which bothered it so,
Was a beautiful pearl, translucent aglow!
This tale has a moral—for isn't it grand
What an oyster can do with a morsel of sand?
What could we do if we'd only begin
With all the things that get under our skin?


# 89.
# Drink from a Running Stream

Howard Hendricks

There was a college student who worked in the college dining hall and who, on his way to work early in the morning, walked past the home of one of his professors. Through a window he could see the light on and the professor at his desk, morning after morning.

At night the student stayed at the library until closing,

and on his return trip again he would see the professor's desk light on. It seemed that he was always poring over his books and notes.

One day, after class, the professor was walking along the courtyard when the student approached him with several lecture questions to clarify. Finally, the student asked, "Would you mind if I asked you a more personal question?"

"Of course not," replied the professor.

So the student asked, "Well, every day I walk by your house and you are so intent at work. What keeps you studying? You never seem to stop."

The professor answered, "Well, you see, I would rather have my students drink from a running stream than a stagnant pool."

# 90.
## "Daddy's Too Tired"

Mark Link, S.J.

The American author O. Henry wrote a story about a young girl whose mother died, leaving her no brothers or sisters. The little girl would wait all day for her father to return home from work. All she wanted to do was to sit on her daddy's lap and cuddle up to him. She was emotionally starved and desperate for affection.

But every night her father followed the same routine. He'd prepare supper, eat, wash dishes and then plop into his favorite chair and read until bedtime.

When his daughter came to sit on his lap, he'd always give the same reply, "Honey, can't you see daddy's too tired. He worked hard all day. Why don't you go outside and play."

The little girl would go outside and play in the street, amusing herself as best she could.

And the inevitable happened. As the girl grew older she began to accept expressions of affection from anyone and everyone who offered them. Finally, instead of playing in the street, she took to living in the street as a prostitute.

When the girl died from an overdose, Peter saw her approaching the gates of judgment. He mentioned to Jesus, "She's a bad one, Lord. Do you know that she's a prostitute and died from a drug overdose? I guess that leaves only one place for her."

Jesus surprised Peter by saying, "Let her into heaven. But when her father's time of judgment comes hold him responsible for what became of her life."

God will be demanding toward those who are responsible for leading others astray. And it may be added that the way we lead others astray is usually not by doing something *to them*. More often it is by failing to do something *for them* that we lead others astray. We will be held accountable and called least in the kingdom of God.

## 91.
## Play Until Good Enough to Teach

Jay Cormier

The great classical violinist Jascha Heifetz, at the zenith of his international concert and recording career, quit in order to accept an appointment as professor of music at the University of California. When asked why he would "pack it in" when he was such a star, the maestro solemnly responded, "Violin playing is a perishable art. It must be passed on as a personal skill; otherwise it is lost."

Then with a bit of a grin, he continued, "I remember my old violin professor in Russia. He said that someday, if I played often enough, I would become good enough to teach."

# 92.
# Tribal Ritual for Antisocial Behavior

## Anonymous

Within the Babemba tribe of South Africa, antisocial or criminal behavior is infrequent, but when it does occur, the tribe has an interesting ritual for dealing with it.

If a member of the tribe acts irresponsibly, he is placed in the center of the village. Work stops and every man, woman and child gather around the accused, forming a large circle. Then, one at a time, each individual, including the children, call out all the good things the person in the center has done in his lifetime.

All his positive attributes, good deeds, strengths and kind acts are recited carefully and at length. No one is permitted to tell an untruth, to exaggerate or be facetious. The ceremony often lasts for several days and doesn't stop until everyone is drained of every positive comment he or she can muster about the person within the circle. Not a word of criticism about him or his irresponsible, antisocial behavior is permitted. At the end, the tribal circle breaks up, a joyous celebration begins, and the person is welcomed back into the tribe.

Apparently this overwhelming, positive influence strengthens the self-esteem of the accused and makes him resolve to live up to the *expectations* of the tribe. For that reason, this ritual is quite rare.

One wonders how a similar ceremony would work in families and other groups.

# 93.
# The Chiefs Go to Washington

Anonymous

Back in the late 1800s the president of the United States invited several Native American Indian chiefs to Washington to discuss the plight of the Indians, and how to preserve the peace on the western frontier.

The chiefs, when introduced to the president, raised their hands, palms outward, and said in a guttural tone, "Chance."

Puzzled, the president composed himself and replied, "Chiefs, don't you mean 'How'"

"We know how," said the chiefs. "We just want a chance."


# 94.
# Polly and Paul's Wedding

David K. Reynolds, Ph.D.

Once upon a time two molecular compounds planned to be married. Miss Polyamide Resin, called Polly, was engaged to Mr. Epoxy Resin, called Paul. They were very happy planning the wedding, but like all couples, they had last-minute jitters.

Polly wondered, "Will he recognize my individuality, my needs?"

Paul, too, wondered, "Will she care about my time, my dreams?"

Both wondered, "Will I still be myself?"

Being molecular compounds of principle, they accepted their reservations and focused on their love and trust, and made a commitment to unite themselves into a larger marital compound. There were still times after the marriage when they thought about their individual identities, but more often they remarked to each other with amazed wonder at how terrific it is to be part of something bigger and more important than the individual parts.

It turned out to be worth giving up some of the self for this greater purpose. In fact, it was downright exhilarating and so self-expanding to do so.

As you guessed, Polly and Paul Resin became epoxy glue when they united their molecules. That means that not only did they stick to each other, but they were also used to hold other parts of the world together. What a very special task that is for them and for you.

## 95.
## Remember Those Who Help

Anonymous

Many years ago two boys were working their way through Stanford University. Their funds became desperately low, and the idea came to them to book the famous pianist, Paderewski, for a recital. They would use the recital revenue to help pay their tuition and board.

The great pianist's manager asked for a $2,000 guarantee. The guarantee was a lot of money in those days, but the boys agreed and proceeded to promote the concert. They worked hard, only to find that they had grossed a mere $1,600.

After the concert the two boys told the great artist the bad news. They gave him the entire $1,600, along with a promissory note for $400, explaining that they would earn the remainder at the earliest possible moment and send the money to him. It looked like the end of their college careers.

"No, boys," replied Paderewski, "that won't do." Then, tearing the note in two, he returned the $1,600 to them as well. "Now," he told them, "take out of this $1,600 all your expenses, and keep for each of you 10 percent of the balance for your work. Let me have the remainder."

Years rolled by—World War I came and went. Paderewski, now premier of Poland, was striving to feed thousands of starving people. There was only one man in the world who could help him—Herbert Hoover, who was in charge of the U.S. Food and Relief Bureau. Hoover responded, and soon thousands of tons of food were sent to Poland.

After the starving people were fed, Paderewski journeyed to Paris to thank Hoover for the relief sent to Poland. "That's all right, Mr. Paderewski," was Hoover's reply. "Besides, you don't remember it, but you helped me once when I was a student at college, and I was in trouble."

## 96.
## Every Part Is Important

Mrs. Floyd Crook

One day a young girl came home from school crying because she had been given only a small part in the school play, while her playmate got the leading role. After drying the girl's eyes, her mother took off her watch and put it in her daughter's hand. "What do you see?" the mother asked.

"A gold band, a watch face and two hands," the girl answered.

Opening the back of the watch, the mother again asked, "Now, what do you see?"

The daughter looked closely at the internal watch mechanism and saw many tiny little wheels, springs and other tiny pieces. "This watch would be useless," the mother explained, "without every part—even the tiny ones you can hardly see."

The young girl always remembered her mother's lesson, and that helped her all through her growing up years to see the importance of even small duties we're asked to perform.

# 97.
# Whose Approval?

## Anonymous

A brilliant young concert pianist was performing for the first time in public. The audience sat enthralled as beautiful music flowed from his disciplined fingers. The people could hardly take their eyes off this young virtuoso. As the final note faded, thunderous applause swept through the audience. Everyone was on his feet, except one old man in the front row. The pianist walked off the stage crestfallen. The stage manager praised the performance, but the young man replied, "I was no good; the performance was a failure."

The manager said, "Look out there! Everyone is on his feet except for an old man up front!"

"Yes," said the youth dejectedly, "but that old man is my teacher."

Whose approval do you seek with the same desire as the young pianist had for his teacher's praise? Are you swayed by public opinion, or the applause of the crowd?

# 98.
# Selfishness Boomerangs

## Anonymous

A very rich businessman died and left his estate to the university from which he had graduated. The instructions in the will, however, directed the administrators to give to his only son that which they wished.

They interpreted the will to mean that the son should get only what they decided to give him. The estate was appraised at $300,000. The administrators got together and decided that they would give the son $10,000.

When their decision was made known, the attorney in charge of probating the will informed the university administrators that they misread the terms of the will. They understood that it was their decision to give the son whatever they decided; however, the will stated that whatever they wished for, the son would get. They wished for themselves $290,000 and, therefore, according to the wording of the will, that is what the son got—that which they wished for themselves. Their selfishness boomeranged.

# 99.
# Discern the Reason for Hostility

Anonymous

Two young men, one an American and the other from India, were roommates at an international conference. During a break in the proceedings, they found themselves talking to each other about religion. The young man from India turned out to be very hostile toward Christianity. The young American tried to discern the reason for his hostility. "Is it something in Jesus' teachings that turns you off?" he asked.

"Oh, no," came the reply, "it's not anything like that. The thing I resent most about Christians is that they do not live like Christians."

# 100.
# What Do You Mean "We"?

Anonymous

A well-known organist was performing a concert on the huge, antique organ in the local Presbyterian church. The bellows were hand-pumped by a boy who was behind a screen, unseen by the audience. The first part of the performance was well received. The audience was thrilled by the organist's ability at the keyboard of the old instrument. After taking his bows and accepting the ovation, the musician walked triumphantly into a side passageway. As he passed the boy he heard him say, "We played well, didn't we, sir?"

The organist haughtily replied, "And what do you mean,'we'?"

After the intermission, the organist returned to his seat at the impressive five-keyboard console and began to play. But nothing happened; not a sound was heard. Then the organist heard a youthful voice whisper from behind the screen, "Say, mister, now do you know what 'we' means?"

# Source Acknowledgments

This book is the fruition of years of reading, listening and transcribing stories from many and varied sources. I thank the authors and publishers who have given their generous cooperation and permission to include these stories in this collection. Further reproduction without permission is prohibited.

Every effort has been made to acknowledge the proper source for each story; regrettably, I am unable to give proper credit to every story. When the proper source becomes known, proper credit will be given in future editions of this book.

THE TOWN DRUNK AND THE PORTRAIT PAINTER
    Anonymous
    Source Unknown

A HALF-BAKED THANKSGIVING (ADAPTED)
    Edward Hays
    *A Pilgrim's Almanac*
    Forest of Peace Publishing, Inc.
    251 Muncie Rd.
    Leavenworth, KS 66048
    Used with permission

GLORY IN BROKENNESS (ADAPTED)
    Eric Hague
    Hong Kong Sketches
    London: Highway Press, 1958

A LITTLE PARABLE FOR MOTHERS
    Temple Bailey
    Source Unknown

GOOD SAMARITAN?
Francis X. Meehan
"Ministry in the Church: A Structural Concern for Justice"
*Review for Religious,* January 1978
via *Storytelling: Imagination and Faith*
Mystic, CT: Twenty-Third Publications, 1984, p. 208

NOW!
Theophane the Monk
*Tales of a Magic Monastery*
NY: Crossroad, 1987, p. 50

PRISONERS OF FEAR
Anonymous
Source Unknown

AGE AND ATTITUDE
Attributed to General Douglas MacArthur
Source Unknown

LEGEND OF THE BLUEBONNET
Anonymous
Source Unknown

STRINGS AND BRIDGES
Anonymous
Source Unknown

THE FIG TREE
David K. Reynolds, Ph.D.
*Water Bears No Scars*
NY: Wm Morrison/Quill, 1987

TAKE A CHILD'S HAND
Anonymous
*Pulpit Helps,* January 1991
6815 Shallowford Road, Chattanooga, TN 37421
Used with permission

A LETTER OF GRATITUDE
Anonymous
Source Unknown

THE SANCTUARY
Mary Alice and Richard Jafolla
*Daily Word,* April 1992, p. 5

THE OLD FAITHFUL WELL
John Sanford
Source Unknown

WORN, FADED AND BEAUTIFUL
Stephanie Whitson
A Cup of Christmas
Nashville: Upper Room, 1988

NO COMMITTEES IN HEAVEN
Msgr. Joseph P. Dooley
*The Joyful Noiseletter,* March 1991
PO Box 895, Portage, MI 49081

RAISING THE BELL
Anonymous
Source Unknown

IT BEGAN IN A TOMB
Mark Link, S.J.
From *Illustrated Sunday Homilies* by Mark Link, S.J.
© Mark Link, S.J., Tabor Publishing, a division of RCL
Enterprises, Inc.
Used with permission

BECOMING A COMMUNITY
Anonymous
*The Boston Globe*, March 1, 1991

AN UNLIKELY PROPHET
Barbara Reynolds
*USA Today*, 4-5-91

EVEN TEACUPS TALK
Anonymous
Source Unknown

LOVE BRINGS TROUBLE
Anonymous
Source Unknown

FINALLY, OUT TO THE BALL GAME
Richard Bauman
*Catholic Digest*, May 1991, p. 65
Used with permission of the author

GREATNESS AND HUMILITY
Anonymous
Source Unknown

PLANS OR BRIDGE?
Anonymous
Source Unknown

COPPER KETTLE CHRISTIANS
Anonymous
Source Unknown

THE FIRST STEP IS COURAGE
Anonymous
Source Unknown

WORLD, MY SON STARTS SCHOOL TODAY!
Abraham Lincoln
*Pulpit Helps,* Feb. 1991, p. 7
6815 Shallowford Road, Chattanooga, TN 37421
Used with permission

WARMTH OF YOUR LOVE
Paul M. Stevens
Source Unknown

LOVE: HEAVEN OR HELL
Anonymous
Source Unknown

WE ARE THREE, YOU ARE THREE (ADAPTED)
Anonymous
*The Song of the Bird*
Anand, India: Gujarat Sahitya Prakash, 1982

PAIN PASSES...BEAUTY REMAINS
Anonymous
Source Unknown

GOD IS LOVE
Anonymous
Source Unknown

COMMENCEMENT AND PARENTS' TRAUMA
Erma Bombeck
*Connections,* May 1991

THE APOSTLE RAISES PIGEONS
Anonymous
Source Unknown

WHY DO I WORK?
Anonymous
Source Unknown

A HANDFUL OF PEBBLES
    Anonymous
    Source Unknown

BIBLE STUDY QUESTIONS
    John De Vries
    Source Unknown

A PARABLE OF CHURCH WORKERS
    Anonymous
    Source Unknown

HIDING BEHIND MASKS
    Anonymous
    Source Unknown

THE TALE OF THREE TREES
    Traditional Folktale
    Source Unknown

WHAT'S UNDER YOUR FEET?
    Anonymous
    Source Unknown

CATHOLICS JUST DON'T GET EXCITED
    Emeric A. Lawrence, O.S.B
    *The Priest*, March 1991, p. 6

LOVE PRODUCES MIRACLES
    Anonymous
    Source Unknown

THE POWER OF THE SAW
    Anonymous
    Source Unknown

POWER OF QUESTIONS
    Anonymous
    Source Unknown

KINDNESS IS STRONGER
>Dr. Norman Vincent Peale
>Source Unknown

THE GRAIN OF RICE
>Anonymous
>*Stories for Telling*
>Minneapolis: Augsburg, 1986, p. 71

LESSONS FROM THE *TITANIC*
>Anonymous
>Adapted from *USA Today*, Sept. 4, 1985

A KIND WORD
>Scott Adams
>Source Unknown

THE WEMMICK
>Anonymous
>Source Unknown

TO TEACH IN PARABLES AND STORIES
>Anthony de Mello, S.J.
>*One Minute Nonsense*
>Chicago: Loyola University Press, 1992, p.112

FACE THE MUSIC
>Anonymous
>Source Unknown

WHERE HAVE ALL THE SERMONS GONE?
>Anonymous
>Source Unknown

LOVE: CREAMY OR CRUNCHY?
>Kathy Noller
>*Catholic Digest*, June 1991

ARE YOU GOING TO HELP ME?
  Mark V. Hansen
  Personal Correspondence
  Used with permission

IF A CHILD LIVES WITH...
  Anonymous
  Source Unknown

TEN COMMANDMENTS OF SPORTS FOR PARENTS
  Anonymous
  Source Unknown

THE OTTER'S CHILDREN
  Jewish Folktale
  *Stories for Telling*
  Minneapolis: Augsburg, 1986, p. 82

SUNDAY SCHOOL'S EASTER LESSON
  Ben Haden
  Source Unknown

A GIVING TREE
  Anonymous
  Source Unknown

THE CHIEF'S THREE SONS
  Anonymous
  Source Unknown

A WARM PREACHING
  Anonymous
  Source Unknown

HOLD MY HAND, FATHER
  Anonymous
  Source Unknown

DISCOVER YOUR POTENTIAL
 Anonymous
 Source Unknown

WHAT IS THE MEANING OF LIFE? (ADAPTED)
 Robert Fulghum
 *All I Really Need to Know I Learned In Kindergarten*
 NY: Villard Books, 1988

TOMORROW
 Anonymous
 Source Unknown

HE WAS A BRICK!
 Anonymous
 Source Unknown

THE PLASTERED CROP
 Anonymous
 Source Unknown

GOD: THE ALPHA AND THE OMEGA
 Anonymous
 Source Unknown

ANOTHER WAY
 Terry Dobson
 Reprinted by permission of Jeremy P. Tarcher, Inc.,
 a division of The Putnam Publishing Group,
 from SAFE AND ALIVE by Terry Dobson. © 1982 by
 Terry Dobson

THE WOODCUTTER AND THE MISSIONARY
 Anonymous
 Source Unknown

PUPPIES FOR SALE
 Anonymous
 Source Unknown

THE SECRET OF LIFE
Anonymous
Source Unknown

SIN IS A SUCKER
Anonymous
*Emphasis,* March 1991, p. 11
PO Box 4503, Lima, OH 45802-4503

DAD, REMEMBER ME
Anonymous
Source Unknown

A BROTHER'S SACRIFICE
Anonymous
Source Unknown

DESIRE BEGINS A FIRE
Anonymous
Source Unknown

YOUR DAILY INVESTMENT
Anonymous
Source Unknown

LIFE REQUIRES A RHYTHM
Anonymous
Source Unknown

TO BE REMEMBERED FOR WHAT? (ADAPTED)
Anonymous
*Think & Grow Rich,* August 1991

THE SECRET OF SUCCESS (ADAPTED)
Clarence DeLoach, Jr.
Source Unknown

QUALITY INVOLVES WAITING PATIENTLY
Anonymous
Source Unknown

THE WATCHMAN
Anonymous
Source Unknown

AM I INDISPENSABLE?
Anonymous
*Leadership,* August 6, 1991

WHAT A FOOL I'VE BEEN!
Anonymous
Source Unknown

THE STORY OF THE OYSTER
Anonymous
Source Unknown

DRINK FROM A RUNNING STREAM
Howard Hendricks
Source Unknown

"DADDY'S TOO TIRED"
Mark Link, S.J.
From *Illustrated Sunday Homilies* by Mark Link, S.J.
© Mark Link, S.J., Tabor Publishing, a division of RCL
Enterprises, Inc.

PLAY UNTIL GOOD ENOUGH TO TEACH
Jay Cormier
*Connections,* September 1991, p. 4

TRIBAL RITUAL FOR ANTISOCIAL BEHAVIOR
Anonymous
"Leadership...with a human touch"
The Economics Press
Fairfield, NJ
Oct. 1, 1991, p. 20

THE CHIEFS GO TO WASHINGTON
    Anonymous
    Source Unknown

POLLY AND PAUL'S WEDDING
    David K. Reynolds, Ph.D.
    *Even in Summer the Ice Doesn't Melt*
    NY: Quill Books, 1986, p. 118

REMEMBER THOSE WHO HELP
    Anonymous
    Source Unknown

EVERY PART IS IMPORTANT
    Mrs. Floyd Crook
    Source Unknown

WHOSE APPROVAL?
    Anonymous
    Source Unknown

SELFISHNESS BOOMERANGS
    Anonymous
    *Pulpit Helps*, October, 1991
    6815 Shallowford Road, Chattanooga, TN 37421
    Used with permission

DISCERN THE REASON FOR HOSTILITY
    Anonymous
    Source Unknown

WHAT DO YOU MEAN "WE"?
    Anonymous
    Source Unknown

# Storytelling Reading List

Abrahams, Roger D., ed. *African Folktales: Traditional Stories of the Black World*. NY: Pantheon Books-Random House, 1983.

*Aesop's Fables*. London: Bracken Books, 1986.

Afasas'ev, Aleksandr, ed. *Russian Fairy Tales*. NY: Pantheon Books-Random House, 1973.

Allison, Christine, ed. *Teach Your Children Well*. NY: Bantam-Delacorte Press, 1993.

Applebaum, Rabbi Morton, and Rabbi Samuel M. Silver, eds. *Speak to the Children of Israel*. Hoboken, NJ: KTAV Publishing House, Inc., 1976.

Arcodia, Charles. *Stories for Sharing*. Newtown, Australia: E. J. Dwyer, Ltd; 1991.

Aurelio, John. *Story Sunday*. NY: Paulist Press, 1978.

———. *Fables for God's People*. NY: Crossroad, 1988.

———. *Colors! Stories of the Kingdom*. NY: Crossroad, 1993.

Ausubel, Nathan, ed. *A Treasury of Jewish Folklore*. NY: Crown Publishers, 1948.

Bausch, William. *Storytelling: Imagination and Faith*. Mystic, CT: Twenty-Third Publications, 1984.

Bell, Martin. *The Way of the Wolf: Stories, Poems, Songs and Thoughts on the Parables of Jesus*. NY: Ballantine Books/Epiphany Edition, 1983.

Benjamin, Don-Paul, and Ron Miner. *Come Sit with Me Again: Sermons for Children*. NY: The Pilgrim Press, 1987.

Bennett, William J., ed. *The Book of Virtues: A Treasury of Great Moral Stories*. NY: Simon & Schuster, 1993.

———. *The Moral Compass: Stories for a Life's Journey*. NY: Simon & Schuster, 1995.

Bettelheim, Bruno. *The Uses of Enchantment.* NY: Vintage Books, 1977.

Bodo, Murray, OFM. *Tales of St. Francis: Ancient Stories for Contemporary Living.* NY: Doubleday, 1988.

*Book of Christmas, A: Readings for Reflection during Advent and Christmas.* Nashville: The Upper Room, 1988.

Bradt, Kevin M., SJ. *Story as a Way of Knowing.* Kansas City: Sheed and Ward, 1997.

Briggs, Katharine. *An Encyclopedia of Fairies.* NY: Pantheon Books-Random House, 1976.

Bruchac, Joseph, and Michael J. Caduto. *Native American Stories.* Golden, CO: Fulcrum Publishing, 1991.

Buber, Martin. *Tales of the Hasidim: Early Masters.* NY: Schocken Books, 1975.

———. *Tales of the Hasidim: Later Masters.* NY: Schocken Books, 1948.

Bushnaq, Inea, ed. *Arab Folktales.* NY: Pantheon Books-Random House, 1986.

Calvino, Italo, ed. *Italian Folktales.* NY: Pantheon Books-Random House, 1980.

Canfield, Jack, and Mark V. Hansen. *Chicken Soup for the Soul.* Deerfield Beach, FL: Health Communications, Inc., 1993.

———. *A 2$^{nd}$ Helping of Chicken Soup for the Soul.* Deerfield Beach, FL: Health Communications, Inc., 1995.

———. *A 3$^{rd}$ Helping of Chicken Soup for the Soul.* Deerfield Beach, FL: Health Communications, Inc., 1996.

Canfield, Jack, Mark V. Hansen, and Barry Spilchuk. *A Cup of Chicken Soup for the Soul.* Deerfield Beach, FL: Health Communications, Inc., 1996.

Canfield, Jack, Mark V. Hansen, Jennifer Read Hawthorne, and Marci Shimoff. *A Cup of Chicken Soup for the Woman's Soul.* Deerfield Beach, FL: Health Communications, Inc., 1996.

Canfield, Jack, Mark V. Hansen, Hanoch McCarty, and Meladee McCarty. *A 4$^{th}$ Course of Chicken Soup for the

*Soul.* Deerfield Beach, FL: Health Communications, Inc., 1997.

Carroll, James. *Wonder and Worship.* NY: Newman Press, 1970.

Cassady, Marsh. *Storytelling: Step by Step.* San Jose, CA: Resource Publications, 1990.

———. *The Art of Storytelling: Creative Ideas for Preparation and Performance.* Colorado Springs: Meriwether Publishing Ltd., 1994.

Castagnola, Larry, SJ *More Parables for Little People.* San Jose, CA: Resource Publications, Inc., 1987.

Cattan, Henry. *The Garden of Joys: An Anthology of Oriental Anecdotes, Fables and Proverbs.* London: Namara Publications, Ltd., 1979.

Cavanaugh, Brian, TOR. *The Sower's Seeds: One Hundred Inspiring Stories for Preaching, Teaching and Public Speaking.* Mahwah, NJ: Paulist Press, 1990.

———. *More Sower's Seeds: Second Planting.* Mahwah, NJ: Paulist Press, 1992.

———. *Fresh Packet of Sower's Seeds: Third Planting.* Mahwah, NJ: Paulist Press, 1994.

———. *Sower's Seeds Aplenty: Fourth Planting.* Mahwah, NJ: Paulist Press, 1996.

———. *Sower's Seeds of Virtue: Stories of Faith, Hope and Love.* Mahwah, NJ: Paulist Press, 1997.

Chalk, Gary. *Tales of Ancient China.* London: Frederick Muller, 1984.

Chappell, Stephen, OSB. *Dragons & Demons, Angels & Eagles: Morality Tales for Teens.* St. Louis: Liguori Publications, 1990.

Charlton, James, and Barbara Gilson, eds. *A Christmas Treasury of Yuletide Stories & Poems.* NY: Galahad Books-LDAP, 1992.

Chinnen, Allan B., M.D. *Once Upon a Midlife.* NY: Jeremy P. Tarcher-Putnam Books, 1992.

Colainni, James F., Sr., ed. *Sunday Sermons Treasury of*

*Illustrations*. Pleasantville, NJ: Voicings Publications, 1982.

Colainni, James F., Jr., ed. *Contemporary Sermon Illustrations*. Ventnor, NJ: Italicus, Inc., 1991.

Colum, Padraic, ed. *A Treasury of Irish Folklore*. 2nd ed. NY: Crown Publishers, Inc., 1967.

*Complete Grimm's Fairy Tales, The*. NY: Pantheon Books, 1972.

Cornils, Stanley, ed. *34 Two-Minute Talks for Youth and Adults*. Cincinnati, OH: Standard Publications, 1985.

Curtin, Jeremiah, ed. *Myths and Folk Tales of Ireland*. NY: Dover, 1975.

Dasent, George Webbe, ed. *East O' the Sun & West O' the Moon*. NY: Dover, 1970.

De La Fontaine, Jean, ed. *Selected Fables*. NY: Dover, 1968.

de Mello, Anthony, SJ. *The Song of the Bird*. India: Gujarat Sahitya Prakash, 1982.

———. *One Minute Wisdom*. NY: Doubleday, 1986.

———. *Taking Flight*. NY: Doubleday, 1988.

———. *The Heart of the Enlightened*. NY: Doubleday, 1989.

———. *One Minute Nonsense*. Chicago: Loyola University Press, 1992.

———. *More One Minute Nonsense*. Chicago: Loyola University Press, 1993.

de Voragine, Jacobus. *The Golden Legend: Reading on the Saints*. Volume I. Princeton, NJ: Princeton University Press, 1993.

———. *The Golden Legend: Reading on the Saints*. Volume II. Princeton, NJ: Princeton University Press, 1993.

Doleski, Teddi. *The Hurt*. Mahwah, NJ: Paulist Press, 1983.

———. *Silvester and the Oogaloo Boogaloo*. Mahwah, NJ: Paulist Press, 1990.

Dosick, Wayne. *Golden Rules: The Ten Ethical Values Parents Need to Teach Their Children*. San Francisco: Harper San Francisco, 1995.

Erdoes, Richard, and Alfonso Ortiz, eds. *American Indian*

*Myths and Legends*. NY: Pantheon Books-Random House, 1984.

Evans, Ivor, ed. *Brewer's Dictionary of Phrase & Fable*. 14th ed. NY: Harper & Row, 1989.

Fahy, Mary. *The Tree That Survived the Winter*. Mahwah, NJ: Paulist Press, 1989.

Farra, Harry. *The Little Monk*. Mahwah, NJ: Paulist Press, 1994.

Feehan, James A. *Story Power!: Compelling Illustrations for Preaching and Teaching*. Originally published as *Stories for Preachers*. Dublin: Mercier Press, 1988. San Jose, CA: Resource Publications, 1994.

Forest, Heather. *Wisdom Tales from Around the World*. Little Rock, AR: August House, 1996.

Frankel, Ellen. *The Classic Tales: 4,000 years of Jewish Lore*. Northvale, NJ: Jason Aronson, 1989.

Giono, Jean. *The Man Who Planted Trees*. Vermont: Chelsea Green Publishing Co., 1985.

Glassie, Henry, ed. *Irish Folk Tales*. NY: Pantheon Books-Random House, 1985.

Graves, Alfred. *The Irish Fairy Book*. NY: Greenwich House, 1983.

Greer, Colin, and Herbert Kohl, eds. *A Call to Character*. NY: HarperCollins, 1995.

Hasler, Richard A. *God's Game Plan: Sports Anecdotes for Preachers*. Lima, OH: C.S.S. Publishing Company, Inc., 1990.

Haugaard, Erik Christian, trans. *Hans Christian Anderson: The Complete Fairy Tales and Stories*. NY: Anchor-Doubleday, 1974.

Haviland, Virginia, ed. *North American Legends*. NY: Philomel Books, 1979.

Hays, Edward. *Twelve and One-Half Keys*. Leavenworth, KS: Forest of Peace Peace Publishing, 1981.

―――. *Sundancer: A Mystical Fantasy*. Leavenworth, KS: Forest of Peace Publishing, 1982.

———. *The Ethiopian Tattoo Shop*. Leavenworth, KS: Forest of Peace Publishing, 1983.

———. *St. George and the Dragon and the Quest for the Holy Grail*. Leavenworth, KS: Forest of Peace Publishing, 1986.

———. *A Pilgrim's Almanac: Reflections for Each Day of the Year*. Leavenworth, KS: Forest of Peace Publishing, 1989.

———. *In Pursuit of the Great White Rabbit: Reflections on a Practical Spirituality*. Leavenworth, KS: Forest of Peace Publishing, 1990.

———. *The Magic Lantern*. Leavenworth, KS: Forest of Peace Publishing, 1991.

———. *The Christmas Eve Storyteller*. Leavenworth, KS: Forest of Peace Publishing, 1992.

———. *Holy Fools & Mad Hatters*. Leavenworth, KS: Forest of Peace Publishing, 1993.

———. *The Quest for the Flaming Pearl*. Leavenworth, KS: Forest of Peace Publishing, 1994.

Henderschedt, James L. *The Magic Stone*. San Jose, CA: Resource Publications, Inc. (160 E. Virginia Street, S–290), 1988.

———. *The Topsy-Turvy Kingdom*. San Jose, CA: Resource Publications, Inc. (160 E. Virginia Street, S–290), 1990.

———. *The Light in the Lantern*. San Jose, CA: Resource Publications, Inc. (160 E. Virginia Street, S–290), 1991.

———. *The Beggar's Bowl: Parables and Short Stories for Spiritual Preaching*. Bethlehem, PA: Faith Journey Creations (PO Box 4219), 1994.

———. *The Hammer Man*. Bethlehem, PA: Faith Journey Creations (PO Box 4219), 1995.

Holdcraft, Paul E., ed. *Snappy Stories for Sermons and Speeches*. Nashville: Abingdon Press, 1987.

Holt, David, and Bill Mooney. *Ready-to-Tell Tales*. Little Rock, AR: August House, 1994.

Hunt, Angela Elwell. *The Tale of Three Trees: A Traditional Folktale*. Batavia, IL: Lion Publishing Corp., 1989 (1705 Hubbard Ave., Batavia, IL 60510).

Jaffe, Nina, and Steve Zeitlin, eds. *While Standing on One Foot: Puzzle Stories and Wisdom Tales from the Jewish Tradition.* NY: Henry Holt, 1993.

Johnson, Barry L. *The Visit of the Tomten.* Nashville: The Upper Room, 1981.

Johnson, Miriam. *Inside Twenty-Five Classic Children's Stories.* Mahwah, NJ: Paulist Press, 1986.

Juknialis, Joseph. *Winter Dreams and other such friendly dragons.* San Jose, CA: Resource Publications, Inc. 1979.

Kronberg, Ruthilde, and McKissack, Patricia C. *A Piece of the Wind and Other Stories to Tell.* NY: Harper & Row, 1990.

———. *Clever Folk: Tales of Wisdom, Wit and Wonder.* Englewood, CO: Libraries Unlimited, Inc., 1993.

Kurtz, Ernest, and Katherine Ketchman. *The Spirituality of Imperfection: Storytelling and the Journey to Wholeness.* NY: Bantam, 1992.

Lang, Andrew, ed. *The Brown Fairy Book.* NY: Dover, 1965.

L'Estrange, Sir Rodger. *Fables of Aesop.* Drawings by Alexander Calder. NY: Dover Publications, 1967.

Levin, Meyer. *Classic Hasidic Tales.* NY: Dorset Press, 1985.

Levine, David, ed. *The Fables of Aesop.* NY: Dorset Press, 1989.

Lewis, Naomi, ed. *Cry Wolf and Other Aesop Fables.* NY: Oxford University Press, 1988.

Lieberman, Leo, and Beringause, Arthur. *Classics of Jewish Literature.* Secaucus, NJ: Book Sales, Inc., 1988.

Livo, Norma J., and Sandra A. Rietz. *Storytelling: Process & Practice.* Littleton, CO: Libraries Unlimited, Inc., 1986.

———. *Storytelling Folklore Sourcebook.* Littleton, CO: Libraries Unlimited, Inc., 1991.

Lobel, Arnold. *Fables.* NY: HarperCollins, 1980.

Loder, Ted. *Tracks in the Snow: Tales Spun from the Manger.* San Diego, CA: LuraMedia, 1985.

Lufburrow, Bill. *Illustrations Without Sermons.* Nashville: Abingdon Press, 1985.

MacDonald, Margaret Read. *Peace Tales: World Folktales to Talk About.* Hamden, CT: Linnet Books, 1992.

*Magic Ox and Other Tales of the Effendi, The.* Beijing: Foreign Languages Press, 1986.

Marbach, Ethel. *The White Rabbit: A Franciscan Christmas Story.* Cincinnati, OH: St. Anthony Messenger Press, 1984.

Martin, Rafe, ed. *The Hungry Tigress: Buddhist Legends & Jataka Tales.* Berkeley, CA: Parallax Press, 1990.

McArdle, Jack. *150 Stories for Preachers and Teachers.* Mystic, CT: Twenty-Third Publications, 1990.

McCarthy, Flor, SDB. *And the Master Answered....*Notre Dame, IN: Ave Maria Press, 1985.

Mellon, Nancy. *Storytelling & the Art of Imagination.* Rockport, NY: Element, Inc., 1992.

Meyer, Gabriel. *In the Shade of the Terebinth: Tales of a Night Journey.* Leavenworth, KS: Forest of Peace Publishing, 1994.

Miller, Donald. *The Gospel and Mother Goose.* Elgin, IL: Brethren Press, 1987.

Minghella, Anthony, ed. *Jim Henson's The Storyteller.* NY: Borzoi-Alfred A. Knopf, Inc., 1991.

National Storytelling Association, The. *Tales as Tools: The Power of Story in the Classroom.* Jonesborough, TN: The National Storytelling Press, 1994.

———. *Many Voices: True Tales from America's Past.* Jonesborough, TN: The National Storytelling Press, 1995.

———. *Storytelling* magazine. NSA, PO Box 309, Jonesborough, TN 37659.

Nelson, Pat. *Magic Minutes.* Englewood, CO: Libraries Unlimited, Inc., 1993.

Newcombe, Jack. *A Christmas Treasury.* NY: Viking Press, 1982.

*Night the Stars Sang, The: The Wonder That Is Christmas.* Tarrytown, NY: Gleneida Publishing Group-Triumph Books, 1991 (by special arrangement with Guidepost Books).

Nomura, Yushi. *Desert Wisdom: Sayings from the Desert Fathers.* New York: Image Books, 1984.

O'Connor, Ulick. *Irish Tales & Sagas*. London: Dragon Books, 1985.

O'Faolain, Eileen. *Irish Sagas and Folk Tales*. NY: Avenel Books, 1982.

Olszewski, Daryl. *Balloons! Candy! Toys! and Other Parables for Storytellers*. San Jose, CA: Resource Publications, 1986.

Parry-Jones, D., ed. *Welsh Legends & Fairy Lore*. NY: Barnes & Noble-Marboro Books by arrangement with B. T. Batsford, Ltd., 1992.

Paulus, Trina. *Hope for the Flowers*. Mahwah, NJ: Paulist Press, 1972.

Pellowski, Anne. *The World of Storytelling*. Revised edition. NY: H. W. Wilson, 1990.

Polsky, Howard W., and Yaella Wozner. *Everyday Miracles: The Healing Wisdom of Hasidic Stories*. Northvale, NJ: Jason Aronson Inc., 1989.

Powers, Isaias, CP. *Nameless Faces in the Life of Jesus*. Mystic, CT: Twenty-Third Publications, 1981.

——. *Father Ike's Stories for Children*. Mystic, CT: Twenty-Third Publications, 1988.

Prather, Hugh, and Gayle Prather. *Parables from Other Planets*. NY: Bantam Books, 1991.

Ramanujan, A. K., ed. *Folktales from India*. NY: Pantheon Books-Random House, 1991.

Robbennolt, Roger. *Tales of Tony Great Turtle*. Leavenworth, KS: Forest of Peace Publishing, 1994.

Seuss, Dr. *Oh, the Places You'll Go!* NY: Random House, 1990.

Schwartz, Howard, and Barbara Rush, eds. *The Diamond Tree: Jewish Tales from Around the World*. NY: HarperCollins, 1991.

Shea, John. *The Spirit Master*. Chicago: Thomas More Press, 1987.

——. *Starlight: Beholding the Christmas Miracle All Year Long*. NY: Crossroad Publishing, 1992.

Simpkinson, Charles, and Anne Simpkinson, eds. *Sacred Stories: A Celebration of the Power of Stories to Transform and Heal*. San Francisco: Harper San Francisco, 1993.

Singer, Isaac Bashevis. *Stories for Children*. NY: Farrar, Straus, Giroux, 1984.

———. *The Image and Other Stories*. London: Jonathan Cape, Ltd., 1985.

Smith, Richard Gordon. *Ancient Tales and Folklore of Japan*. London: Bracken Books, 1986.

Stanton, Sue. *Boston and the Feast of St. Francis*. Mahwah, NJ: Paulist Press, 1994.

Stoddard, Sandol. *The Rules and Mysteries of Brother Solomon*. Mahwah, NJ: Paulist Press, 1987.

Stone, Richard. *The Healing Art of Storytelling*. NY: Hyperion, 1996.

Stromberg, Bob. *Why Geese Fly Farther Than Eagles*. Colorado Springs: Focus on the Family Publications, 1992.

Sutherland, Zena, and Myra Cohn Liningston, eds. *The Scott, Foresman Anthology of Children's Literature*. Glenview, IL: Scott, Foresman and Co., 1984.

Tazewell, Charles. *The Littlest Angel*. Nashville: Ideals Publishing, 1946.

Thoma, Clemens, and Michael Wyschogrod, eds. *Parable and Story in Judaism and Christianity*. Mahwah, NJ Paulist Press, 1989.

Thompson, Stith. *The Folktale*. Los Angeles: The University of California Press, 1977.

Valles, Carlos G., SJ. *Tales of the City of God*. Chicago: Loyola University Press, 1993.

Vecsey, Christopher. *Imagine Ourselves Richly: Mythic Narratives of North American Indians*. San Francisco: HarperCollins, 1991.

Ward, Benedicta, trans. *The Sayings of the Desert Fathers*. Kalamazoo, MI: Cistercian Publications, 1975 (revised 1984).

Weinreich, Beatrice Silverman, ed. *Yiddish Folktales*. Translated by Leonard Wolf. NY: Pantheon-Random House, 1988.

Wharton, Paul, ed. *Stories and Parables for Preachers and Teachers*. Mahwah, NJ: Paulist Press, 1986.

White, William R., ed. *Speaking in Stories*. Minneapolis: Augsburg, 1982.

———. *Stories for Telling*. Minneapolis: Augsburg, 1986.

———. *Stories for the Journey*. Minneapolis: Augsburg, 1988.

Wiesel, Elie. *Souls on Fire: Portraits and Legends of Hasidic Masters*. NY: Summit Books, 1972.

———. *Somewhere a Master: Further Hasidic Portraits and Legends*. NY: Summit Books, 1981.

Wilde, Oscar. *The Happy Prince and Other Fairy Tales*. NY: Dover, 1992.

———. *The Fairy Tales of Oscar Wilde*. NY: Henry Holt & Co., 1993.

Wood, Douglas. *Old Turtle*. Duluth, MN: Pfeifer-Hamilton Publishers, 1992.

Wrede, Patricia A. *Book of Enchantments*. NY: Jane Yolen Books/Harcourt Brace, 1996.

Yolen, Jane, ed. *Favorite Folktales from Around the World*. NY: Pantheon Books-Random House, 1986.

Zipes, Jack, ed. *Spells of Enchantment: The Wondrous Fairy Tales of Western Culture*. NY: Viking-Penguin, 1991.

———. *Aesop's Fables...and 200 other famous fables*. NY: Signet Classics-Penguin, 1992.

# Theme Index

| Theme: | Story Numbers: |
|---|---|
| Evangelization | 27, 44, 64, 67, 73 |
| Expectations | 84, 92 |
| Faith | 8, 28, 42, 57, 64, 65, 77, 79 |
| Faith/Works | 73 |
| Family | 2, 4, 12, 30, 45, 52, 57, 58, 59, 65, 78, 90, 92 |
| Farming | 76 |
| Father/Son | 57, 63, 65, 77 |
| Father's Day | 57, 90 |
| Fear | 7, 19, 28 |
| Fellowship | 44 |
| Forgiveness | 66 |
| Fortitude | 4, 57 |
| Franklin, Benjamin | 70 |
| Freedom | 28 |
| Friendship | 2, 23, 34 |
| Funeral | 4, 16, 55 |
| Generosity | 20, 30, 62 |
| Genesis | 17, 52 |
| Gifts/Talents | 3, 15, 16, 18, 25, 27, 45, 49, 62 |
| God | 34, 57, 65, 71 |
| God's Will | 42, 53 |
| Golden Rule | 21, 23, 66, 73, 83, 87, 92, 95 |
| Good Friday | 41, 42 |
| Good Samaritan | 5, 48 |
| Gospel Witness | 27, 40, 44, 55, 67, 70, 73, 99 |
| Graduation | 35 |
| Gratitude | 2, 13 |
| Greatness | 10, 25, 91 |
| Greed | 5, 9, 21, 62, 98 |
| Handicaps | 45, 74 |
| Haydn, Franz Joseph | 25 |